THE MYSTERY OF
BAPTISM
in the Anglican Tradition

KENNETH STEVENSON

MOREHOUSE PUBLISHING

Morehouse Publishing
P.O. Box 1321
Harrisburg, PA 17105

Morehouse Publishing is a division of the Morehouse Group.

Printed in the United States of America

Cover design: Corey Kent

Cover art: Art Resource/Eric Lessing: The Baptism of Christ by Joachim Patinir

A catalog record for this book is available from the Library of Congress.

0-8192-1774-3

Contents

vi   *Contents*

Preface

In the autumn of 1976, Trevor Collins, then Vicar of Boston, asked me to write an historical drama about baptism for a confirmation class. I have used that drama in various forms over the years in several places as an increasingly important teaching aid. Then in the spring of 1988, Colin James, Bishop of Winchester and Chairman of the Church of England Liturgical Commission, and Alec Graham, Bishop of Newcastle and Chairman of the Doctrine Commission, invited me to prepare a paper for the House of Bishops on the various theological issues connected with baptism, including confirmation, personal renewal, and reconciliation. As I went on at the same time to study the eucharistic theology of the seventeenth-century Anglican divines, I suppose it was inevitable that I should turn my hand to writing about the mystery of baptism as well.

This book is a result of these strands coming together. It has been written in the conviction that the Anglican tradition is a living reality that can be fed abundantly by the writers placed under scrutiny here. I have sought to do so through the dual perspectives of twentieth-century experience and historical theology. A few of these writers have been studied for their baptismal theology before, but most of them have not.

Many people deserve my thanks in the production of this book. H. R. McAdoo and Christopher Cocksworth read the draft and made many useful comments. My Chaplain, Andrew Davis, was a frequent foil to many ideas as they occurred and were tested. Bryan Spinks, Colin Bradley, Stephen Sykes, Geoffrey Rowell, Rowan Williams, Donald Allchin and David Stancliffe gave valuable encouragement and assistance. Peter Robinson's anthropological perspectives proved to be of great value. My senior colleagues, Michael Yorke, Graeme Knowles, Mervyn Banting and Michael Jordan assured me of more support than perhaps they realized. I am also grateful to the former Sion College Library (a tragic loss for many a scholar-pastor); the Dr Williams's Library, and the Thorold and Lyttleton Library, Winchester, for access to many necessary books; and to the Muniment Room, Westminster Abbey, for access to the Thorndike manuscripts and for generously photocopying some of his unpublished sermons. Jean Maslin and Julie Hale patiently produced the completed script. But by far the biggest thanks must go to my family, to my wife Sarah, and to Elisabeth, Kitty, James and Alexandra, and our two border terrier puppies, who all put up with a distracted companion – and kept laughing.

It has been a joy to put these thoughts together as Bishop of a diocese whose Cathedral – after recent extension and reordering – is a robust and elegant testimony to the centrality of the font in the life of the Church. This book is dedicated to those who are baptized and confirmed here, and their pastors. Their faces are an inspiration in the covenant of grace.

Kenneth Stevenson   *Petertide, 1997*

I

Conversation with History

It is a sense of fracture or a sense of imprisonment that sends historians back to the archives, the memoirs, the tape-recorded voices. Yet this relation between loss and the imagination is full of irony. History has less authority than memory, less legitimacy than tradition. History can never speak with the one voice that our need for belonging requires.[1]

When were you baptized? I cannot remember my own baptism in the same way that I can remember where I was when I heard that President Kennedy had been assassinated or that Mrs Thatcher had resigned. But I have done some digging into the family archives and have put together something of my personal history. I discovered that I was baptized on the afternoon of Saturday 17 December 1949 in St Peter's Church, Musselburgh. The family used to attend that church and the Rector was one of my godparents. The service was taken by Canon John Ballard, who had just seen my father through to becoming a Reader in the diocese of Edinburgh. The church building, moreover, became a familiar sight in later years when we moved further away, because it stands on what was then the main road into Edinburgh. I am told that my baptism was only attended by family and close friends. There was a virtual repeat performance for my sister in the spring of 1954, and according to one piece of family folklore I fell asleep towards the end of the reception afterwards because I went around emptying everyone's sherry glasses.

Then in the summer of 1958 it was arranged that my brother and I should be confirmed along with the rest of the group of young people in the congregation at St Anne's, Dunbar. To save my brother and me a journey on a weekday evening over a period of weeks, the Rector kindly came and prepared us both for confirmation. I remember his kindness and his carefulness in explaining all manner of things to do with Christian faith and worship. He was always ready to answer questions. And he patiently put up with our interruptions.

All this led to the confirmation service on Saturday, 20 December 1958 in St Anne's by Kenneth Warner, Bishop of Edinburgh. I remember the service well, particularly because it was postponed a week at a day's notice; one of the border clergy had died and the Bishop had to go and take the funeral. My brother and I were given our confirmation presents – a watch each – a week in advance, to make up for the disappointment. The service left quite an impression on me. We all sat in the front pews on the north side of the central aisle, and our families and friends huddled around us and sang the hymns lustily. I recall noting how odd it was that the Bishop *sat* in his chair, even for the hymns. He wore a red and gold cope and my father acted as his Chaplain. As we came up one by one the Rector, Edmund Ivens, called out our names. I remember the touch of the Bishop's hands. I remember too being told to wait after the service for the Bishop to come and give us our confirmation card. The wait seemed like an age. But he eventually appeared, wearing just a cassock, and told us that the card was 'a record of our confirmation'. We duly went up and had a less formal contact with him, and then we went home, with our families.

But there was one rather strange event that day. We gathered in the church in the morning for a rehearsal, and suddenly there was a baptism. One of the candidates had not been baptized, and now he was to be baptized surrounded by his fellow confirmation candidates! *We* were the congregation as no family or friends seemed to want to be there. I was asked to be one of the servers in order to assist the Rector through the service, even though I did not have much of a clue as to what was happening. But the other Reader in the parish who presented this young lad for baptism took care to find the service for each one of us in the Prayer Book. I remember him distinctly saying to himself in each case 'the baptism of those of riper years' – and adding humorously, 'nothing to do with orange and apples'. At the service, the candidate stood against the font, and the Rector poured water over his head with a mother-of-pearl shell. It all seemed like a routine that was being gone through in as dignified a way as possible. But it left an impression. Finally, on the next morning, we all took communion at the early Eucharist, a quiet service in the traditional style, and from that time onwards our Christian lives progressed and regressed with the passage of years.

It is indeed a 'sense of fracture' as well as a mild 'sense of imprisonment' (to borrow from Ignatieff) that sends me back to the family memoirs as I reconstruct those events from remembered conversations with those who took part. There is for me an inevitable sense of loss, for it is the past, a past that has changed almost beyond recognition, not least over matters of liturgy. Liturgical practice over baptism and confirmation does still vary a great deal but I would hazard a guess that the scenario described above would be different now. The child of practising Anglican parents today would be baptized during a Sunday morning Eucharist in St Peter's, Musselburgh. The Bishop of Edinburgh would have come to St Anne's, Dunbar on a Sunday morning to celebrate what is often regarded as the richest form of Eucharist, one in which baptism and confirmation take their full place. There

would be one service, not three. And the young lad would
be baptized by the Bishop – for all to see. I expect, too, that
the candidates for confirmation would nowadays be prepared
not only by the local Rector but by lay people as well.

But to borrow again from Ignatieff, 'History can never
speak with the one voice that our need for belonging requires',
and that is very much the theme of the pages that follow.
Christian belonging is about many things. It is about the
welcome at the back of church. It is about the encouragement
of family and friends. It is about the capacity to ask God the
difficult questions that are at the time unanswerable when
tragedy strikes, rather than giving up on him altogether.
Christian belonging has a special and primal place at the font,
in the rough and tumble of a community getting to grips with
the Christian faith through its young, in the confirmation
preparation, and in the regular celebration of the Eucharist.
The fragmented picture of my own passage through these
various rites may be somewhat out of date in contemporary
terms but it has nonetheless been the way in which Christians
have been nurtured for many centuries. Indeed, the fragmented nature of Christian experience is very much a given
aspect of our lives. We can never arrange things so neatly
that God is gift-wrapped, cut-priced, and easily available.

This is what makes sacraments so fascinating, particularly
the two main sacraments, baptism and Eucharist. In water
and in bread and wine the Church is given the equipment to
wash in rebirth and to feed her members. So often in history
the Church has had to walk something of a tightrope between
saying (on the one hand) that sacraments are important, vital,
gifts of God, actions of the Church, in which certain important things happen, and (on the other hand) saying that they
are part of a wider whole, the means for the journey of faith,
patterns of divine life in which we can live and grow, events
to focus on but not to confine God within them.

*   *   *

It is easy to see golden ages in the past and to approach the past with our own particular agendas. Looking back on what I now know of my own baptism, the events on the day of my own confirmation – complete with a rehearsal that ended up with the baptism of a candidate of 'riper years', and the confirmation itself, followed by the communion at the Eucharist the next day – I can see a kind of jumble, a collection of fragments from history. There is the old established norm that goes back to the Middle Ages, whereby infants are indeed baptized, catechized subsequently by the local priest, and confirmed by the bishop. But I can also see the signs of that scheme breaking down in that strange adult baptism at which all I seemed to do was lift the Rector's cope as he stretched out his right hand to pour the baptismal water. In the Anglican divines whom we shall be looking at later, there seemed to be no settled scheme either. There were attempts to justify an inherited system that was in need of adaptation. Many of them delved into the ancient past for inspiration for their ideas and even for the justification of their ideas. It was a scheme that was on the move though the questions they faced were often different from ours. As with today's inheritance, often the way the liturgy is celebrated and what it contains mirrors the issues of the time. Some old churches provide ample evidence of this variety through the sixteenth and seventeenth centuries.

For example, Langley Chapel in Shropshire was probably built in 1564 but with some additions later. It is a simple, small building erected for the residents of the nearby Langley Hall, which has since been pulled down. The interior of the church expresses the ideals of the Puritan approach to worship, grounded in simplicity. There are pews and benches for the congregation, and two pulpits, one of them movable. At the east end there is a communion table round which the congregation will have gathered on those Sundays when the sacrament was celebrated. But there is no evidence of any font. I would hazard a guess that if I had been born at Langley Hall at the time, I would have been baptized in the church in a basin set up on a table for that purpose. Such a practice was frowned upon, no less than moving the old fonts from their position near the door, by the bishops from the beginning of the reign of Queen Elizabeth onwards.[2] Proof enough that it was common practice!

Then there is the church of St Mary, Acton Burnell, which was built about 1270–80 by Richard Burnell, who was Bishop of Bath and Wells and Lord Chancellor to King Edward I. He enjoyed royal favour and had the right 'to crenellate' his family house next to the church, i.e. to turn it into a castle. Everything in this church is of the best. Near the entrance to the church there is an octagonal font. Fonts sometimes had eight sides, not just for geometrical unity but to symbolize the eighth day of the week as the day of the new creation and baptism as the expression of that new birth. On the corner which faces outwards to the rest of the church, there is some stiff foliage carved into the stonework. This is no mistake but a gently eye-catching trick to point to that eighth day. It is easy to imagine the Prayer Book rite celebrated around this font in the context of the offices of Morning and Evening Prayer. Here is the Reformed but still Catholic Church of England using its medieval architectural inheritance and attempting to make the baptism service more *public*, as the title of the service in the Prayer Book suggests.

Then there is, by contrast, the Church of the Holy Trinity at Minsterley, an unusual building which was completed in 1689. The font was originally placed opposite the south door. Its proportions are small by medieval standards and it stands lower than many of its medieval counterparts. One could imagine an adult standing over such a font and being baptized with the form for those 'of riper years' which was only introduced to the Prayer Book in 1662.[3]

Such is the way that three churches in different parts of

Shropshire might have been used for the sacrament of baptism. But they might have been used differently. The Langley baptism could have taken place at home, again around a basin. At Acton Burnell, there could have been a parson in the reign of Elizabeth I who was a devout follower of the Puritans. He therefore would *not* have used the font at the back of the church but would have set up a basin at the head of the nave. Perhaps he would have left out those parts of the service of which he disapproved, for example, the promises by the godparents and the sign of the cross. As to confirmation, this took place when the Bishop performed his Visitation, because there was no explicit direction that confirmation should be held in *church*. It is conceivable that when the faithful of Minsterley were confirmed by the Bishop of Hereford, the service happened outside. Moreover it was even known for churches to have *two* fonts, one in the old position and another in a more accessible place, as in Herefordshire at Sutton St Michael during the time of the Commonwealth.[4]

In the pages that follow, we shall be looking at the writings of nine theologians from the end of the reign of Queen Elizabeth I through to the time of Charles II, each of whom has important things to say about how baptism is celebrated liturgically, about how theology relates to worship. It is a short time span but it is rich in debate and controversy that have a direct bearing on many of the issues facing the Churches today. For each one of them what we believe and exactly what we do – and don't do – about it at the font matter a great deal. Michael Ignatieff's 'sense of fracture' and 'sense of imprisonment' do indeed send the historian back to these archives, these memoirs. Unfortunately the tape-recorded voices are not available, but the material is richly textured and rewarding to ponder. The historian does so knowing full well that the past certainly does not speak with one voice, and we shall delve into this material realizing that our need for belonging in the Christian Church is one that is never ultimately satisfied.

Although they cover between them a great deal of ground, each has a particular insight that leaps to the enquiring twentieth-century eye. 'Is baptism inward or outward?' asks William Perkins. 'How is baptism a means of sharing in the life of God?' asks Richard Hooker. Baptism is the opening of heaven above Christ, as Lancelot Andrewes preached at Whitsun in 1615. God's foreknowledge of us is the dominant theme in the baptism poems of George Herbert. 'What happens to the unbaptized?' asks John Bramhall. Richard Baxter sees us all as disciples of Christ at the font. Jeremy Taylor spreads baptism through human experience as a pattern of 'holy living'. Our profession of Christian faith is always counter-balanced by God's redemption in our hearts and lives, as Simon Patrick eloquently testifies. And Herbert Thorndike sees the covenant of grace between God and humanity begun sacramentally at the font and continued at the only sacrament which bears fruitful iteration, the Holy Communion.

This is the collective memory of what came to be called Anglicanism that we shall tap. It is made up of a combination of ingredients, in which context plays a significant role, through an ordered liturgy which has its own balance of change and stability. And the criteria for that continuity and change are invariably a very Anglican combination of scripture, tradition and reason, always in tension when addressing specific concerns, and always trusted to work towards a solution. It is a rich, varied, and vivacious read, and one in which we may be able to find some explanations of how we in the late twentieth century have arrived at where we are now. It may also beckon us not only to nurture our sense of tradition, but to be sustained by it, to the point of looking yet more profoundly at how we can build a more secure future.

2

Setting the Scene

I once attended an ecumenical conference at theological college at which one of the speakers was Bishop Alan Clark, who was the first Roman Catholic Co-Chairman of the Anglican Roman Catholic International Commission. The 'Agreed Statement' on the Eucharist had just been first issued.[1] He was about to address us on that seemingly intractable problem, eucharistic dialogue between Anglicans and Roman Catholics.

Earlier that morning he had walked across from the theological college into Salisbury Cathedral to say his prayers. He sat still for a while and looked around and wondered at the beauty and the sense of continuity and discontinuity in the building. The medieval Gothic architecture remained. But there were important changes, which expressed the way in which the Church of England had absorbed aspects of the Reformation in the sixteenth and seventeenth centuries. There had been change and development since then as well. And he could enjoy the way in which the two sister Churches, Roman and Anglican, were drawing closer together. We were being encouraged by a new atmosphere of dialogue and co-operation. In company with other Churches also we were responding to what the Spirit was saying to the Churches in our own age.

One particular expression in his talk to us stuck in my mind. He referred to the Reformation as 'an explosion of ideas'. Explosion indeed it was. And for many people, a necessary explosion. It was an explosion that for many sought to change the outward face of the Western Church without losing its inner heart.

Among the issues debated was the place of baptism. After all, how we understand this sacrament of entry into the Church – and how we perform it liturgically – are bound to be questions that affect the kind of Christian community that we are. A particular Anglican characteristic has tended to explore the relationship between sacraments as they are experienced in human lives and as they are celebrated as objective actions of the Church. This has often nowadays been called 'thick description' by anthropologists.

At the Reformation, these issues were indeed hotly debated all over Europe. They were debated not only for what they were said to *teach* – theology – but also for the way in which they were *done* – in worship. Thus, they adjusted the theology and liturgy of baptism. It was quite an operation to work out criteria for doing so. Calvin in France and Switzerland and Luther in Germany, followed by others elsewhere, including Thomas Cranmer in England, stripped the liturgy down. The pouring of water over the head of the child was to be central. Confirmation was abolished, though where it survived – initially only in England – the emphasis came to be focused as much on the candidates' profession of the Christian faith, as on their blessing and strengthening in the power of the Holy Spirit by the Church.

Of course, the scene was far more complicated than that. For neither Calvin nor Luther was the journey straightforward.[2] But they and their colleagues, together with Thomas Cranmer in the first two English Prayer Books, inherited the medieval pattern of Christian initiation that persisted in all its fragmentation down to recent times. Baptism was primarily for those in infancy, and parents were expected to have their children baptized. Catechesis and first communion followed as the child got older and was able to understand more. The first two Prayer Books of 1549 and 1552 presuppose that scheme, adding a form of private baptism for when the child is dangerously ill, and a simple form of confirmation by the bishop. The form of baptism for those 'of riper years' was the main addition to the Prayer Book in 1662; it was added probably for two reasons, the Church's mission in North America, and the numbers of people who were not baptized as infants during the time of the Commonwealth when the Prayer Book was proscribed and the influence of those wanting to delay baptism into adulthood was in some places strong.[3] The other significant addition was the active profession of faith by the candidates at confirmation – all grist to the mill of those who wanted Christian *commitment* expressed in the liturgy.

Catholic ceremonies, like anointing with oil and elaborate ways of blessing the baptismal water, were abolished – although Cranmer did retain a blessing of the water, another indication of conservatism in England. Luther retained the sign of the cross before baptism, whereas Calvin got rid of it. Luther retained godparents, whereas Calvin got rid of them also, and required the *parents* of the child to make the promises at baptism. Already a varying picture is emerging. The Reformation did not proceed in a uniform manner at all. When, after the death of Edward VI in 1553, Mary Tudor reigned as a Catholic monarch again, it was inevitable that those budding churchmen who took the chance to escape to mainland Europe should encounter a more distinct style of Reformed Christianity in centres like Geneva and Zürich than they had known back home in England. When they returned at the beginning of the reign of Queen Elizabeth I from 1558 onwards, many of them became valuable allies of the new monarch in her opening years. Together they faced the Catholic inheritance, and one of the results is that English Christianity became a matter of debate and controversy.

All these changes were not solely in the interests of simplifying the liturgy. They were about theology as well. Medieval

Catholic teaching about baptism was to the effect that baptism is for the washing away of original sin. The Reformers challenged this, but in different ways: what about the centrality of the work of Christ on the cross? What about sins committed after baptism, which would not be dealt with automatically in the confessional? Baptismal theology therefore shifted in the same way as teaching about the Eucharist, towards views that tried to hold in some kind of tension the action of the Church in faithful obedience to the Lord's command (on the one hand), and *faithful reception* on the part of the believer (on the other). Insofar as there is any discernible theological scheme, it concentrates on the way the symbol of water functions in relation to the gift of salvation.

In his work on Calvin's eucharistic theology, Brian Gerrish suggests three models. We shall return to them later on, when we come to assessing the work of our nine writers. They approximate to three views of what sacraments do.[4]

The first is symbolic *memorialism*. This can be identified most immediately with the radical Swiss Reformer, Ulrich Zwingli. Sacraments are pledges of God's goodwill to us. Baptism becomes an action that is a memorial of what Christ has already done for us. This is an exaggerated view, which suspects the language of sacramental efficacy. Faithful reception is the dominant part of the equation.

Then there is symbolic *parallelism*, a view that can be identified with Zwingli's successor at Zürich, Heinrich Bullinger. A careful distinction is made between outward and inward baptism. As Bryan Spinks has suggested, 'they are not identical, but neither are they totally unconnected. They are simultaneous and parallel.'

Thirdly, there is symbolic *instrumentalism*, a view which Gerrish identifies with John Calvin himself, and it can also be found in the writings of Martin Luther. The sacraments are 'visible words' (to use Augustine's well-known tag); they are not bare signs, but consist of the sign and what is signified together. The water of baptism conveys the gift of salvation in the sacrament itself; faithful reception begins from that point. As we shall see, Anglican teaching tends strongly towards this third view, because it is faithful to tradition and at the same time allows ample scope for the basic Reformation emphasis on human appropriation.

The principal way in which debate and controversy in England operated – and still does today in world-wide Anglicanism – is the almost *endemic* manner in which this particular style of Reformed Christianity is determined to face both ways. The Church of England is Catholic, but it is not Roman Catholic. It is Reformed, but it is not like the Reformed Churches of the Continent. From some of the writings which will be discussed later, it is apparent that there were elements in this English Church that also found an increasing amount of inspiration in the Greek Fathers and the Eastern Christian traditions. In this connection, one name stands out particularly strong, that of Lancelot Andrewes. The extraordinary characteristic of this Church of England is that traces of this endemic tendency to be both Catholic and Reformed are to be found in virtually every service of *The Book of Common Prayer*. As far as baptism and confirmation are concerned, a good example is in the following prayer, which first appears in 1549 and survives thereafter:

Almighty and immortal God,
The aid of all that need, the helper of all that flee to thee for succour, the life of them that believe, and the resurrection of the dead:
We call upon thee for this infant that he, coming to thy holy baptism, may receive remission of his sins by spiritual Regeneration.
Receive him, O Lord as thou hast promised by thy well

beloved son, saying, ask, and ye shall receive; seek,
and ye shall find; knock, and it shall be opened unto
you:
So give now unto us that ask; let us that seek find; open
the gate unto us that knock; that this infant may
enjoy the everlasting benediction of thy heavenly washing, and may come to the eternal kingdom which thou
hast promised by Christ our Lord. Amen.[5]

This prayer has a curious origin. Archbishop Thomas Cranmer will have known it from his Catholic days as the prayer
used in the baptism rite when putting salt in the candidate's
mouth. Much earlier, Augustine uses the image of knocking
on the door when exhorting candidates to come forward for
baptism. This probably inspired the composition of the prayer
in the first place, for when it was originally written, probably
in the sixth century (if not earlier), the ceremony of the giving
of salt took place some time before the baptism, and was part
of the rites associated with the final part of the catechumenate
– the group of people preparing for baptism. If they were
mainly adults, or if a high proportion of them were adults,
then it made a great deal of sense to 'ritualize' the last stages
in preparation for baptism.

The prayer in its original form is marked by two main
features. One is that it was originally a prayer in the singular,
uttered by the priest almost as a personal petition over
the candidate. This Cranmer changed to the more normal
plural 'we'. Secondly, the prayer has at its heart the
teaching of Jesus about asking, seeking, and knocking (Matt.
7:7–8; Luke 11:9–10). In other words, the prayer as adapted
by Cranmer places the candidate – and the congregation iden-
tifying with the candidate – on the threshold of the Christian
life.

This is probably why the prayer was a winner with Cranmer, and to a lesser extent with Luther, who abbreviated it

for his baptismal rite. All those rich periods near the start – 'the aid of all that need, the helper of all that flee to thee for succour, the life of them that believe, and the resurrection of the dead' – express the sheer dependence upon God that is at the heart of the deepest classical traditions of Christian prayer. After the quotation from Matthew's Sermon on the Mount about asking, seeking, and knocking, and turning those into petitions on behalf of the whole congregation, the prayer ends by asking for 'the everlasting benediction of thy heavenly washing' and 'the eternal kingdom which thou hast promised'. Cranmer, like the other Reformers, took to prayers that quoted the Bible. And he also liked prayers that had a strongly devotional flavour to them. In retrospect, therefore, it seems hardly a surprise that it should find itself near the start of Cranmer's baptism rite.

Another aspect of Reformed liturgies in which the Prayer Book shares is the use of *scripture*. In the later Middle Ages, the passage about Jesus blessing the children was introduced as a kind of warrant for infant baptism (Matt. 19:13–15). Cranmer, however, followed Luther and changed the reading to the corresponding one in Mark's Gospel (Mark 10:13–16). He seems to have been interested in the passage as a basis for baptism as far back as about 1537.[6] The version in Mark is more forceful. In Mark, where Jesus shows his displeasure to the disciples when they try to stop the children coming to him, he adds the extra teaching about receiving the Kingdom of God as a little child, and he takes the children up in his arms before he blesses them. At a time when the more radical reformers were questioning infant baptism, it was important for the liturgy to be seen to be defending it. It is interesting to note that when the form of baptism for those of 'riper years' was framed for the 1662 Prayer Book, the corresponding scripture passage was Nicodemus before Jesus, with the telling command from Jesus that those who were to enter the Kingdom of Heaven must be born again of water and the spirit (John 3:5), a passage much used by many Reformers (and others before them) to defend the necessity of baptism.

It is easy with the benefit of hindsight to underestimate the sheer impact of these prayers written for the first time in a language understood by most people, and using scripture passages from vernacular translations of the Bible. Both those factors were bound to make the activity of creating fresh liturgies and reforming old ones an exciting venture both on the part of those drafting the prayers as well as for those on the receiving end among the church congregations. In both the prayer discussed earlier and in the use of a scriptural warrant for baptism, the English Church was showing its desire to look in both those directions, namely to stand for continuity with its Catholic inheritance, and for discontinuity in the face of Reformation developments.

The debates and controversies built up their own head of steam. Two are of particular importance and both date from the reign of Queen Elizabeth I. The first was occasioned by John Jewel (1522–71) and concerned the Church of England and the Roman Catholic Church. Jewel was probably one of the most brilliant men of his time. A convinced Protestant, he was ordained in 1550 or 1551 and did much to forward the cause at Oxford. He hoped to survive under Queen Mary Tudor but soon realized that his life was in danger. He fled Oxford in March 1555 and spent the next four years in Frankfurt, Strasbourg, and finally Zürich. Such personal contacts as he made there, which included John Knox at Frankfurt and Peter Martyr at Strasbourg, led him to think carefully and clearly about his own theological position. In January 1560, soon after his return to England, he was consecrated Bishop of Salisbury. He is probably one of the most famous occupants of that See. High on the agenda of the Church of England as it settled down to a new monarch and another phase of life as a Reformed Catholic Church was the need to state with clarity and erudition that it was indeed a true part of the Catholic Church.

In 1562, Jewel published his *Apology of the Church of England*, which was a lengthy defence against the Roman Catholic Church. It was written in Latin and an English translation by Lady Ann Bacon, wife of Sir Nicholas Bacon, Lord Keeper of the Great Seal, appeared in 1564. When you defend yourself against someone else, you must expect a rejoinder. This came in the form of *An Answer to M. Jewel's Challenge*, which was written by Richard Harding and published also in 1564. Harding had been a Canon of Salisbury during the reign of Mary Tudor and had been deprived of his post for his Catholic position in 1559. He therefore had little reason to love the new Bishop, and his description of him as *Mr.* Jewel was an eloquent enough admission of his own view that the man was not really ordained at all. Jewel fought back in the following year with his *Reply to Harding's Answer*, and each wrote a subsequent set of rejoinders. Each work is longer than its predecessor.[7]

In the *Apology* Jewel states that baptism is a sacrament, and it is to do with the remission of sins and the redemption through the work of Christ. He insists that no-one should be prevented from being baptized, because they are fallen and in need of God's forgiveness.

Harding accuses Jewel of demoting sacrament to be 'no more but a token or sign'. And he goes further into the attack by saying that baptism does not depend on the faith of the giver or receiver but on the power and virtue of the sacrament in God's promise. Jewel counters this in his *Reply* by agreeing on the sacramental nature of baptism, but emphasizes the need for godparents when babies or young children are being baptized, and he laces his discussion with references to the Fathers, including Augustine and Jerome. It is clear, for example, that Jewel agrees with Augustine (and many of the

Fathers) when he identifies the water of baptism as being in the place of the blood of Christ.

> We say that baptism is a sacrament of the remission of sins, and of that washing which we have in the blood of Christ; and that no person which will profess Christ's name ought to be restrained or kept back therefrom, no, not the very babes of Christians, forsomuch as they be borne in sin, and do pertain unto the people of God.[8]

The second controversy, by contrast, concerned the Church of England and those who wanted to take her in a more Reformed direction. It will be noted that Calvin abolished such patristic practices as godparents and the sign of the cross. These, however, were retained in the 1552 Prayer Book, and not abolished when, with some small alterations, that book was re-issued in 1559 at the start of Queen Elizabeth's reign. The signing of the cross at baptism was the only example left of many more signs of the cross from the medieval rites, and it was accompanied by a formula which expressed Christian discipleship in terms of combat: 'we receive this child into the congregation of Christ's flock, and do sign him with the sign of the cross, in token that hereafter he shall not be ashamed to confess the faith of Christ crucified, and manfully to fight under his banner against sin, the world, and the devil, and to continue Christ's faithful soldier, and servant unto his life's end.'[9] Cranmer was retaining a traditional custom which went back to the earliest time and was underscoring its significance: baptism is baptism into the cross of Christ, it is about discipleship, it is about witness to him in newness of life. As for godparents, although in 1552 they no longer had to lay their hands on the head of the child after baptism, they were still an integral part of the service. In 1549, the questions at baptism were addressed directly *to the child* for the godparents to answer, following medieval practice, whereas in 1552, the questions were addressed direct *to the godparents*, which served to highlight the role of god-parents in a stronger way than previously.

There were, however, many for whom Cranmer's liturgical arrangements had not gone far enough. Baptism by midwives survived from the pre-Reformation era in an age of infant mortality, but many railed against it as archaic and meaning-less. The signing of the cross, along with the position of the font, remained contentious. As early as 1562, there was an unsuccessful attempt in Convocation to make the sign of the cross optional.[10]

In 1572, an 'Admonition to Parliament', by John Field and Thomas Wilcox, called for the abolition of the blessing of the water, promises by the godparents, and the signing of the cross; and it recommended that there should be a proper sermon at baptism, and that *parents* should present the child and make confession of the faith on its behalf. The Second Admonition called for the abolition of confirmation altogether.[11]

Things could not be left to rest like this. John Whitgift was Master of Trinity College, Cambridge, and Vice-Chancellor of the University. He had already forced the leading Puritan, Thomas Cartwright, who was wholeheartedly behind the Admonitions, out of his Cambridge Fellowship and Professor-ship. He wrote at once an *Answer to the Admonition* (1572), and Cartwright wrote a *Reply* (1573–4); Whitgift wrote a *Defence of the Answer* (1574), whereupon Cartwright wrote a *Second Reply* (1575–7). The two of them fought hammer and tongs, Whitgift defending with ever greater fervour the Prayer Book practices, and Cartwright criticizing them with ever increasing conviction. As John New has observed, two different view of the Church and sacraments were at logger-heads. Whitgift, loyal Protestant though he was, believed in an inclusive Church, where sacraments are effective signs of nature transformed by grace, whereas Cartwright believed in a gathered Church, founded by God, whose prevenient grace was so strong that sacraments had less impact.[12] Defence of the issues these two fought over was to carry on for the next ninety years – and beyond.

From these two episodes we can see the Church of England defending itself against Roman Catholicism on the one hand, and also entering into strong debate with those who did not think that the English Church had gone far enough in Reformation. Moreover, the position of Cartwright and his colleagues was shared by many, including a group of Scottish Presbyterian ministers who fled to England in 1584, and made a list of twenty-two objections to the English *Book of Common Prayer*, of which six concern baptism. The list could have been drawn up by the Admonitioners or Cartwright himself: baptism by midwives in necessity, baptism and Eucharist in private places, questions at baptism to the god-parents, the sign of the cross at baptism, confirmation by the bishop, and the view that children who were baptized somehow had all things necessary for their salvation.[13]

With such a strong debate going on, it was inevitable that the English Church would have to look thoroughly and repeatedly at the theology and practice of baptism. On the subject of confirmation, it was not as if the Prayer Book scheme was functioning properly. In 1587 Robert Cawdrey pointed out that most bishops had not been performing confirmations at all for the past twenty-nine years – meaning right from the beginning of the reign of Elizabeth I.[14]

As we turn now to look at each one of our nine writers, we need also to bear in mind the very different people they were and the different means of communication which they adopted. Perkins writes popular treatises for the common man. Richard Hooker writes a single *magnum opus* into which he poured so much of himself, a work needing to be sipped and mulled over carefully. Lancelot Andrewes preaches brilliant sermons, packed full of ideas and images, but is always able somehow to see things whole. George Herbert writes poems with a simple directness almost unequalled in that remarkable century, as every line – especially if full of monosyllables! – hits its own particular point. John Bramhall tackles a particular topic of conversation at a dinner party – the unbaptized – and cannot stop himself from trying to have the last word. Jeremy Taylor turns the deprivations of internal exile into a God-given chance to pour out lavishly his own utterances on the holy life for the ordinary person. Richard Baxter, ever the self-taught loving pastor, writes at ever greater length in practical exhortation to discipleship. Simon Patrick transforms a sermon on baptism into his first published work, always a love-child for an author. Herbert Thorndike perhaps turns the art of rich and repetitive discourse into its own art form, which is reflected in his sermons too.

To these we must now turn.

3

Inward or Outward?

William Perkins (1558–1602)

Is baptism an inward or an outward reality? I have heard many people talk often in quite contrasting ways to this effect. I can remember a person speaking to me with great earnestness about the day when she 'became a Christian'. It was the result of a special, heart-warming occasion when the Christian faith in all its truth and conviction suddenly made sense to her. There had been a time of hostility – or extended apathy – towards the Church. Then, as usually happens, a friend was involved. A conversation passed that important watershed when people begin to talk about what is really important to them. A powerful experience at a church service convinced her that Christianity was the key to all her longings.

But what of her previous life? The answer to that question could be given in a number of ways. Perhaps there was no Christian background whatever, in which case she was now baptized as a believing adult. Perhaps she was baptized as an infant by parents who took her along to church, in the hope that she would one day make a more conscious commitment to the Christian faith, whereas in fact she had perhaps discarded Christianity before 'Sunday School' (or its equivalent) could beckon her. Perhaps, again, her parents were barely practising Christians, and so this new experience of Christianity pushes her infant baptism back into the recesses of the barely important, even the trivial.

Another way I have heard the question, 'Is baptism inward or outward?' answered was as follows. It consisted of a series of dates, along the lines of how I chronicled my own baptism and confirmation earlier. On that interpretation, I am baptized and born again of water and the Spirit at that same moment. I am given nurture by the Christian community, leading up to my confirmation, where I reaffirm my baptismal vows and receive the gift of the Spirit through the hands of the bishop. Everything that the Church does relies on that basic premise that God acts through the sacraments and the sacramental rites, and human experience responds accordingly. Whereas the person who was converted as an adult experiences that inward baptism and it remains important to her for the rest of her life, the other person relies on the outward baptism in the sacraments of the Church, and any important experiences of faith and commitment that occur at later points interpret that baptism.

Not everyone would respond in one or other of those rather cut-and-dried ways. But the question nonetheless has to be asked: how far do we rely on our experience, and how far do we rely on the actions of the Church? It is not an issue that is new, for we find it in the New Testament when the apostles Peter and John went to Samaria and prayed for new converts that they might receive the Holy Spirit, after they had been baptized in the name of the Lord Jesus. (Acts 8:14 ff.) Indeed, it could be said that the apostle Paul himself experienced an inward baptism at his conversion which was rapidly followed by his outward baptism at the hands of Ananias (Acts 9).

This is the kind of world in which baptism has had to live and adjust to different climates of belief and practice. For example, in the fourth century, there is ample evidence that baptism was deliberately led up to by careful catechesis and dramatic liturgy at the celebration of baptism at the Easter Vigil.[1] On the other hand, by the later Middle Ages, baptism in the West was usually an automatic process. Confirmation had become an episcopal rite, and from the late thirteenth century confirmation in England was made a requisite for Holy Communion in order to gain full recognition.[2]

As people reflected on their religious experience, they took on more and more of a new life. The late medieval mystics are a clear example. Walter Hilton (who died in 1396) wrote a classic called *The Scale of Perfection* in which he takes for granted the sacramental effects of baptism but is much more interested in the relationship between what we would call spiritual renewal and the practice of penance, private confession.[3] If you were to ask some of Walter Hilton's contemporaries who read his work the difference between inward and outward baptism, they would probably have needed the question explained to them. They would not have thought in those terms. But I would hazard a guess that they would remain confident about the effectiveness of the outward baptism given by the Church but would then wax more than lyrical about the different ways in which 'inward baptism' is experienced in Christian prayer, contemplation, and living. There is some evidence to suggest that Hilton, perhaps uniquely for his time, built an important bridge between the theological and sacramental traditions of the Church, and the nurturing of the lives of lay folk through knowledge of the scriptures and a spirituality accessible to them. That inevitably makes him a significant figure in the pre-Reformation scene, not least for the strand of Reformation piety often referred to as 'Puritan'.

Inward and outward baptism form perhaps the most significant part of the teaching of William Perkins.[4] Sadly, Perkins is little known these days, partly because he has been overshadowed by the work of Richard Hooker and Lancelot Andrewes, whom we shall look at in subsequent chapters. But the truth of the matter is that he was a far more popular communicator in his own time than either of the other two figures. For example, his *A Golden Chain*, which first appeared in 1590, went through nine editions in thirty years. It was translated into Dutch and German, and other works by him were translated into many other languages, including Spanish and French.

Perkins was born in Warwickshire and went up to Christ's College, Cambridge in 1577, where he associated with the more strongly Protestant part of the English Church, often called Puritan. After graduating, he obtained a Fellowship at Christ's College, and acted as a volunteer chaplain at Cambridge jail. He was soon made Lecturer at Great St Andrew's, which was a poor parish, attended by members of the university as well as townsfolk. Lecturers were appointed by the parishes, not the bishop, and the post was effectively that of a senior curacy with the particular task of preaching. There he stayed until his death, and we are told that his preaching and pastoral ministry became part of Cambridge folklore. There are indications that he was not entirely happy with the Prayer Book and this may explain why he remained a Lecturer for the duration of his ministry, since he could thereby avoid questions being asked about his attitude to, for example, vesture and kneeling for the reception of Holy Communion. Perkins represents a more moderate form of Puritanism than that of Thomas Cartwright. He was determined to stay firmly within the Church of England in order to change it from inside. He has had his successors in many generations since, who have been intent on blowing fervour and understanding into the historic formularies of the Church as these are actually celebrated in parish churches.

There are three particular works that tell us about his views on baptism. The first – a very popular one – is called *A Golden Chain or The Description of Theology*.[5]

A Golden Chain demonstrates Perkins' style as a clear and fluent writer. Very near the start comes the statement that 'theology is the science of living blessedly forever'.[6] He then discusses God – his nature and his life, his glory and blessedness, the Trinity, God's works – and moves on to man and his fall, original sin, Jesus Christ, the two natures in Christ, and the work and ministry of Christ.

At this stage, he turns towards the sacraments, and in four chapters (31–4) discusses what he calls the 'covenant of grace', the sacraments in general, and baptism and the Lord's Supper.[7]

For Perkins, the Covenant of Grace – as for many of the Reformers – is a biblical image to describe the relationship of free grace between God and humanity which is sealed in Christ. The covenant's purpose is 'to manifest that righteousness in Christ whereby the whole law is fully satisfied and salvation attained'.[8] He goes on to describe it as 'the conduit pipe of the Holy Ghost'. Those who knew about architecture at the time will have warmed to that image of the conduit pipe, much beloved, too, of Lancelot Andrewes,[9] because this was a way of ensuring that clean water could be available to townsfolk, at least those who lived in the right place.

He defines a sacrament as 'that whereby Christ and his saving graces are by external rite signified, exhibited and sealed to a Christian man'.[10] And he distinguishes the two words of institution, the commandment ('go into the whole world baptizing them in the name etc.' – Matt. 28:19), and the promise ('I baptize thee in the name of the Father and of the Son and of the Holy Ghost'). Then comes the crunch: 'the covenant of grace is absolutely necessary to salvation . . . but a sacrament is not absolutely necessary, but only as it is a prop and stay for faith to lean upon.'[11] Here, Perkins departs from Catholic tradition – and also from Jewel and Whitgift – most obviously, because he sets the covenant of grace above the sacraments. This is most clearly to be seen in the table which he gives to describe the outward and the inward baptism (see pp. 28–29).

Perkins wants to have his baptismal cake and eat it! The inward and the outward are so clearly delineated that he gives the impression of wanting to put a wedge between the inward and the outward – and yet he wants to hold them together. The outward baptism, as he explains in the accompanying text in *A Golden Chain*, consists of three parts, namely the sprinkling or dipping in the water, continuance in water, and arising from water. The person being baptized is to do two things: give his body to be washed, and receive that washing.[12] He does not seem entirely happy with what the outward baptism does in relation to the inward. 'The party baptized doth receive the internal washing which is by the blood of Christ, or at least it is offered unto him.' He switches from dying-and-rising to the image of rebirth in order to counter the claims of Anabaptists, who would only baptize adults: 're-baptising is at no hands to be admitted, for as in natural generation man is only once born, so it is in spiritual regeneration'. He is more confident, however, about the inward baptism and its relationship to the forgiveness of sins:

> For although baptism be but once only administered, yet that once testifieth that all men's sins past, present and to come are washed away . . . Therefore baptism may be truly termed the sacrament of repentance and, as it were, a board to swim upon when a man shall fear the shipwreck of his soul. Last of all, see thou never rest till such time as thou have a feeling of that renewing power signified in baptism: namely the power of Christ's death mortifying sin and the virtue of his resurrection in the renovation of the spirit.[13]

Perkins defines baptism as 'a sacrament by which such as are within the covenant are washed with water in the name of the Father, the Son and the Holy Ghost . . . These are either of riper years or infants.'[14] Those of riper years can be

The Sacramental Union

The External Baptism

Things sensible: water

Actions sensible of him

Minister to wash the unclean body in the name of the Father etc.

Sprinkling or dipping in the water etc:

Continuance in water

Arising from water

Receiver to

Give his body to be washed

Receive that washing

of the Parts of Baptism

The Union of the Figure and the thing Signified	Christ's blood and figuratively all Christ }		Things spiritual }	Inward baptism
	1. Remission of sins and imputation of Christ's justice 2. Mortification of sin by the force of Christ's death }			
	The progress and continuance in mortification	God's spiritual washing is regeneration }	Actions spiritual and inward }	
	Vivification and sanctification thro' Christ's resurrection			
	To consecrate himself to God and to forsake flesh, devil, and world	Receiver		
	To feel the inward washing of the spirit			

baptized on their own promises but infants are baptized on the basis of their parents' faith. They bring their children into the covenant, even though their age prevents them from actually believing. The solemn covenant is simply this: God receives the believer with favour, and the baptized promise to acknowledge and worship him.

When discussing the methods of baptism, Perkins is aware of the lavish use of water in antiquity and suggests this as appropriate for those of riper years, but follows many of the Reformers in allowing sprinkling for small babies because of climate and the possible danger to health.[15]

The second work of Perkins is his Commentary on Galatians.[16]

By its very nature it is a more academic work, though the style is as clear and flowing as ever. His treatment of baptism arises from Galatians 3:27, 'For as many of you as were baptized into Christ have put on Christ.' Once again Perkins tackles the outward and the inward straight away, perhaps occasioned by the reference to 'putting on Christ'. He states: 'the outward baptism without the inward is not the mark of God's child, but the mark of the "fool that makes a vow, and afterwards breaks it" (Eccles. 5:3)'.[17] But he says that baptism is not only a sign but a seal and takes the opportunity of discussing baptism under no fewer than seven headings.

First there is the *name*. The Pharisees had religious washings; God also had appointed certain washings in the Old Testament. In the New Testament baptism was a washing by water to seal the new covenant, but it was also used as a metaphor for any grievous cross, or the bestowing of extraordinary gifts. It was also used in connection with ministry in the Church. Then he says – almost in contrast to what he propounded earlier – that 'the inward washing is conferred with the outward washing'.

Secondly, the *matter* of baptism. Should there be dipping or sprinkling? (The Prayer Book directed dipping as a norm.)

He realizes that climates vary. What is appropriate in the north of Europe is not appropriate elsewhere, as he pointed out in *A Golden Chain*. Water is the sign, the thing signified is nothing less than Christ himself our mediator. Then, repeating what he had to say in *A Golden Chain*, he says that 'the dipping of the body signifies mortification, or fellowship with Christ in his death: the staying under the water signifies the burial of sin; and the coming out of the water, the resurrection from sin, to newness of life (Romans 6:4).'[18]

Thirdly, the *form* of the sacrament. In Matthew 28:19, Christ makes his promise and seals his promise by baptism. We need, therefore, to become disciples and to 'lay hold of the promises of God and the confirmation thereof by the sacraments'. We shall be seeing later how he disposes of the sacramental rite of confirmation but here he clearly places confirmation in the context of personal growth in the life of Christ.

Fourthly, the *ends* of baptism. It is a pledge in respect of our weakness, a sign of Christian profession before the world, a means of our first entrance into the visible Church, and a means of unity.[19] The Puritans place great stress upon the outworking of Christian discipleship in daily life and this part of the discussion should not be underestimated. Perkins may not be confident about the objective character of baptism as a sacramental event but he is certainly clear about its need as a focus for Christ's presence in the unfolding life of the forgiven Christian.

Fifthly, the *efficacy* of baptism. Perkins asks various questions. One, 'Does baptism forgive all sins and the whole of the life of a man?' Against tradition, which requires penance for certain sins, Perkins insists that 'the covenant of grace is everlasting ... therefore baptism is not to be tied to any time'. Two, 'Does baptism abolish original sin?' Against the Catholic view, which insists that it does, Perkins observes that 'though actual guilt be taken away, yet potential guilt remaineth, namely as aptness in original sin, to make men guilty'.[20] This comes near the modern view that original sin is a 'bias to the bad'. Three, 'How does baptism confer grace?' It does so like a king's letter that saves the life of a malefactor; or the outward washing is a token and pledge of the inward. 'He that useth the sign aright, shall receive the thing signified.' And he goes on: 'it is not an instrument having the grace of God tied unto it, or shut up in it; but an instrument to which grace is present by assistance in the right use thereof . . . a moral and not a physical instrument.' Here is the outward and the inward again doing creative battle in the sacramental sphere. Perkins' heart seems to be on the side of faithful reception of the sacrament rather than what the sacrament does in itself. Hooker, as we shall see, insists that the sacraments are both moral *and* physical, in order to safeguard their centrality, and to prevent them becoming optional, or, worse still, visual aids. Four, 'Does baptism imprint a character or mark in the soul?' Again, it is almost as if Perkins wants to go further than he can: 'Baptism is a means to see this mark in us; because it is the laver of regeneration.'[21] For him it cannot therefore have an indelible character. Five, 'Is it necessary to be baptized?' In view of what he said in *A Golden Chain*, that sacraments are a prop to faith, the answer must surely be a mild 'no'. It is 'necessary in part'. 'The want of baptism . . . does not condemn . . . The children of believing parents are born holy.' And yet, in discussing John 3:5: 'baptism makes men visible members of the Church; and regeneration by the spirit makes them true and lively members!'[22]

Sixthly, the *circumstances* of baptism. Only ministers should baptize, because 'private teaching and ministerial teaching are distinctive in kind'. The intention is there to baptize and even if the minister is not a preacher, it is still a true baptism. The efficacy of the sacrament depends not on the will of man but on the will of God. As far as the persons being baptized are concerned, 'men of years that join themselves to the true Church are to be baptized, yet before their baptism, they are to make confession of their faith, and to promise amendment of life.[23] Further, 'infants of believing parents are likewise to be baptised . . . and are in the covenant of grace. They are the children of God because in their conception and birth God begins to manifest his election. Infants do have faith, and parents have faith on their behalf, a position to which I rather incline.' Baptism must only be administered once, in the public assembly of the congregation, and 'the whole congregation is to make profit by the enarration of the institution of baptism.'

This leads him on to his seventh and final section, on the *use* of baptism. 'Our baptism must put us in mind, that we are admitted and received into the family of God.' At this point Perkins propounds a powerful baptismal spirituality. To contemplate one's own baptism means looking at the life that is past, in examination and confession and deprecation, towards the life that is to come, in the purpose of not sinning, and in endeavour to perform a new obedience to Christ, and it is 'a storehouse of all comfort in the time of our need'. Perhaps most powerfully of all he states, 'if a man would be a student of divinity, let him learn and practise his baptism . . . The best commentary to a man's own self is his own baptism.'[24]

He then relates the gift of being adopted sons of God to putting on the garment, putting on Christ, as in the verse which provoked this whole discussion (Gal. 3:27). We are made one with Christ by the gift of Christ to us, by Christ's gift to himself of his giving of his 'spirit' to make us conformable to himself in holiness and newness of life. Putting on Christ makes us aware of the nakedness of creation and the nakedness of our hearts.[25] To uncover our nakedness at the same time brings out our shame and our need to be clothed by Christ himself. But the trouble is, as he notes, many of us have worn this garment very loosely. And he ends, 'though we be clothed with Christ in baptism, yet we must further desire to be clothed upon.' In other words, there is more and more yet to know and experience in the Christian life.

Finally, we must take a brief look at Perkins' *Problem of the Forged Catholicism.*[26] This consists of a discussion of Roman Catholic beliefs and practices to which Perkins takes exception. He devotes a few pages to confirmation, which he simply identifies with the use of chrism. He shows an historical perspective which reads almost like a twentieth-century tract. He knows that oil was used in the ancient world in bathing and that is how it was introduced into the baptism rite. Oil was commonly used, Perkins knew, as an extra ceremony at baptism, but he did not regard it as a separate sacrament, as did Roman Catholics. He looks back to the Early Fathers who 'did not hold their Chrism and imposition of hands to give grace by the work wrought'. The imposition of hands is no more than a prayer over the person and it was performed by the bishop because the bishop was the normal president of the liturgy. Finally, 'of the form of confirmation we find nothing in scripture: and if we betake ourselves to tradition we shall find great ambiguity and variety hereof in the Fathers'. His Reformation priorities enabled him to see through Catholic practice, with the benefit of a better knowledge of antiquity.

Clearly, Perkins has no use for confirmation! Even if he did, it would become a spanner in the works of the outward/ inward view of baptism that he propounds so comprehensively in *A Golden Chain* and the Commentary on Galatians. Confirmation is nothing but the confirmation of the believers as they grow up in the Christian faith and mature in holiness and newness of life. Perkins' approach to baptism, moreover, is strongly pastoral and linked to the dying and rising of Christ (Rom. 6:3 ff.). If there is a weak New Testament ingredient, it is the Holy Spirit. In taking such a line, Perkins follows Luther and Calvin, and English Puritans such as Cart-wright and many others. As we shall see, the necessity of confirmation was considerably debated.

What are we to make of Perkins' theology of baptism? Were he alive today, he would probably be saying exactly the same things. Baptism is an external rite which is about inward renewal. For the conscious believer, profession of faith must be made at the font, but the believing parents of infants can make that profession on behalf of their children. The rite is stripped down in its essentials to the water: going in, staying there, and arising from it. There is no blessing of the water, nor signing with the cross. The celebration must be before the public assembly, who will profit by it, as they witness the baptism of new Christians and are confronted by their own baptism. Confirmation by the Bishop is not necessary. Receiv-ing the sacrament of the Lord's Supper is confirmation in itself for the conscious believer.

The strength of this position lies in its attention to faithful reception. But its weakness is to be seen in that ambiguous relationship between sacrament and human experience that we saw both in *A Golden Chain* and in the Commentary in Galatians. Perkins is sure that sacraments are necessary. But because baptism is a sacrament of growth, and he allows it to children, and human beings are sinful and fall away, he cannot quite bring himself to say that it actually does some-thing objective. This is the dilemma of a sacramental theology which starts with human experience and draws the tradition exclusively into that orbit.

In his *Art of Prophesying* (1592),[27] Perkins shows yet again his love for simplicity and clarity, and his suspicion of con-trived complexity. 'Artis etiam celare artem: it is also a point of art to conceal art.'[28] One of his rare gifts was to make complex things seem simple, clear, and related.

Liturgically, we can only guess at Perkins' preferred or

actual practice. He would have dispensed with godparents, and their promises, as well as the sign of the cross and the blessing of the water. He would have simplified the rite in other respects and he would have ensured a fully *public* rite, with a proper sermon, and a liturgy suitably adapted for those of 'riper years'. He would also have admitted to communion on the basis of growing faith, and no more. All these changes would serve to stress faithful reception and appropriation of the sacraments of baptism and Eucharist, and collectively would play down their objective character.

How, then, does he affect our twentieth-century debate about the inward and outward baptism? He is understated, to the point of being weak, on the role of the Holy Spirit. Sacraments are a prop to faith, secondary to the covenant of grace itself. Provided that faith is seen as the gift of God and located in a living way through the Christian community down the ages, then the sacraments of baptism and the Lord's table are secure. But once that faith migrates into the individual choice of the believer, the sacraments become visual aids and little more. The lasting legacy of Perkins is that he wanted to hold the outward and inward baptism together. The way he did it may not be entirely convincing, but when he says in his commentary on Galatians that 'the best commentary to a man's own self is his own baptism', that inward baptism is challenging and vibrant beyond all words – and experiences.

4

Sharing in the Life of God

Richard Hooker (1554–1600)

Boston Parish Church is one of the largest churches in Britain. It was built in the fourteenth century and the tower is 270 feet high. It is an unmistakable feature of the skyline and because of the flat countryside of fenland Lincolnshire, it can be seen for miles around. As the visitor enters the church the first sight to be seen is a large font, set on a series of steps, designed by the famous Victorian architect, Augustus Pugin, and given to the church in 1853.

The font has been put to all different kinds of uses. It has been used for dramatic moments in Christmas Carol services, at the Easter Vigil, and for occasions during special services when the choir gathers round to sing from it. There is so much space that the font makes its own impact. At Christmas, the crib has often been placed there, so making the point that the rebirth of the human race began – in a sense – with the birth of Jesus as the Christ in Bethlehem.

I have celebrated many baptisms there. At first, it felt rather strange, standing up so high, and I do remember one occasion when I almost slipped as I came down the steps with a young baby immediately after baptizing him. I have heard many criticisms of this particular font. Some have said it is too large. Others have said it is out of date, presumably because the architect was Pugin. Others again have said that it is ugly. But no-one can doubt its sheer impressiveness, surrounded as it is by such an open Perpendicular Gothic interior.

Not to put too fine a point on it, one simply cannot avoid this font. It gets in the way. And one of the reasons why it has aroused comment over the years is that it poses in its own way the question, what are we to do with our fonts? Is the font a kind of expression of God? God either gets in the way or he has moved around his church-buildings to suit passing fashions, like a kind of convenience food. These are questions that have a bearing on what we do with church interiors today and they were questions that were alive in the sixteenth and seventeenth centuries as well.

If the font is a silent expression of God in our midst, then perhaps the question needs to be asked, how do we share in the life of God in the first place? If we come to be washed at the font, and go on to feed at the altar, and if we keep going back to that font every time we witness a baptism, then the font's very 'God-likeness' becomes its own question.

There are three answers that are supplied by the New Testament, and in each case they have baptismal overtones. First of all, there is the image of being part of the Body of Christ. 'Now you are the body of Christ and individually members of it' (I Cor. 12:27).

To be part of the Body of Christ is not just to be part of a club of like-minded people – and very often they are not like-minded at all! – but it is to *share* at the deepest level in the common humanity of other people, and to do this *in Christ*. For the deeper that one enters into a relationship with someone else, the more fully we are tested, and faced with our own humanity. That is what it means to be part of Christ's Body. Christ identifies himself with us so fully that we are able to identify ourselves with him. Moreover, this 'Body of Christ' exists in history, but in a way that is far deeper than the mere historical manifestation of that Body in a particular place and at a particular time. Whenever I presided at a service of baptism when I served as a priest in Boston in the late

1970s, I was forcefully reminded of this truth simply by facing in any direction away from the font as I stood there. My voice echoed hither and thither in that vast nave. I couldn't fail to get a strong sense of a Body of Christ that reached down through history, not only back into the past but forward into the future.

The second image takes us away from sharing to the more allusive one of *abiding*. We come across this word no fewer than seven times at a particular stage in the Fourth Gospel, when Christ describes himself as 'the true vine'. Shortly after he describes himself as the true vine, he says, 'Abide in me, and I in you. As the branch cannot bear fruit by itself, unless it abides in the vine, neither can you, unless you abide in me' (John 15:4). Just as there is mutuality in the image of sharing, so there is with abiding. To abide is to remain, to rest, and it has resonances of permanence rather than activity. It is as if Christ were saying to his followers, I am the source of your life, and I am ready to stay with you forever. Every time I stood at that font, I had, too, a strong sense of that abiding presence, not just because of the size and proportions of Pugin's design, but because of the sanctity of the building and its atmosphere. Visitors would come and go, individual members of the Body of Christ vary from one generation to another, but this church building would go on and on – or at least for as long as we could keep it up!

The third image is *repentance* – 'repent, and believe in the gospel' (Mark 1:15). For many people, repentance is a big word that might mean saying sorry. But it means much more than that. At so many baptism services down the ages, the candidate or the sponsors have been asked, 'Do you repent of your sins?' The word 'repent' was often accompanied by a dramatic physical gesture which symbolized exactly what the word originally meant. In ancient times, candidates for baptism would often face west and renounce the deeds of darkness, and then turn through 180 degrees to the east to profess their faith in Christ. To repent is to undergo a change of mind – not in the intellectual sense, but in the sense of the whole person going through that turning round, that re-alignment, that re-focusing, that renewal, which is itself a work of God, not our own. So many times when I stood at that font, I looked west through the huge space under the tower, and imagined the wealthy Hanseatic merchants who built the place and the kind of world they inhabited. Then I turned east, and looked up through the even vaster spaces of the nave towards the altar, and had in my mind's eye the Lord Christ, accepting that repentance, daily, weekly, yearly, by the century.

Right at the end of the life-time of the New Testament, one of the writers expresses all these truths in the rich theological expression – 'partakers of the divine nature' (2 Pet.1:4). And of all the writers in the seventeenth century, this approach to sacraments in general and baptism in particular is most strongly exemplified by Richard Hooker.[1]

From a literary and theological point of view, the contrast between Perkins and Hooker could not be greater. Perkins' prose is plain and ordinary, whereas Hooker's is more literary in style, and less easily accessible. Perkins' career was primarily as a preacher, whereas Hooker forsook the Temple Church in London, where he was locked in controversy with his Puritan colleague Walter Travers,[2] in order to become a country parish priest, where he could write.

Hooker was an Elizabethan in every sense of the word. He was born just four years before the accession of Elizabeth and died on 2 November 1600, just a few years before her death. Before his time at the Temple Church in London, he had been an aspiring scholar at Oxford, where he befriended Edwin Sandys, son of the Bishop of London, and George Cranmer, nephew of the former Archbishop. It was John Whitgift, now Archbishop of Canterbury, who ensured his appointment as Master of the Temple in 1585, and it is likely that Hooker had been identified as a rising star. But he soon tired of being centre-stage in London, with a colleague like Walter Travers who was so different in every way. The last two posts he held were as Sub-Dean of Salisbury and Rector of Boscombe in 1591, and from there he moved only four years later to Bishopsbourne in Kent in the Canterbury diocese. His great work *The Laws of Ecclesiastical Polity* flowed from his pen during these last years. The first four books appeared in 1593, while he was still at Salisbury, and the fifth, by far the longest, was published in 1597. (The remaining books appeared much later: the sixth and eighth in 1648, and the seventh in 1661. While it is clear that they represented Hooker's completed thought, they may have been prepared for publication from a semi-completed text.)

Sharing in the life of God is perhaps one of the dominant motifs of Hooker's writings, for near the beginning of Book I of the *Laws*, we come across the following statement:

> No good is infinite, but only God: therefore he our felicity and bliss. Moreover desire leadeth unto union with what it desireth. If then in him we are blessed, it is by force of participation and conjunction with him. Again it is not possession of any good thing that can make them happy which have it, unless they enjoy the thing wherewith they are possessed. Then are we happy therefore when fully we enjoy God, even as an object wherein the powers of our soul are satisfied, even with everlasting delight; so that although we be men, yet being unto God united we live as it were the life of God.[3]

This is a fundamental statement of the nature of humanity's yearning for God, and God's response to humanity. We desire God for he is our fulfilment. And desire draws us into 'participation and conjunction with him', in other words to share with him and to be joined with him. But this sharing and being joined to him is more than a psychological uplift or assent to attractive ideas. It is a deep connection between ourselves and God which is made by Christ, through the Spirit, and effected in the public worship of the Church, above all in the sacraments. The soul's ultimate satisfaction, therefore, is to be united with God, and that union is a way of sharing in God's life itself.

As John Booty remarks, 'the straightforward interpretation of Book V is to view it as a defence of the Book of Common Prayer against the objection of the Puritans who contended that it was full of superstitious practices'.[4] The opening chapters tackle head-on the Admonitions to Parliament of 1572, that Puritan manifesto for the reform of the Church of England, in which Thomas Cartwright was a leader, and for which he was nearly arrested before he fled the country.

The structure of *Laws V* in its published form of 1597 is a sheer delight. Hooker begins by dealing with superstition, the general principles for the use of a set liturgy, and the use of church buildings, and then goes on to discuss the need for public prayer, with some discussion of the offices of Morning and Evening Prayer.

Chapters 50–68 are the sacramental heart of the book. The remainder deals with the liturgical year, the pastoral offices, and questions of ordination and the discipline of the clergy. In this central portion, Hooker discusses the doctrine of the Trinity, the incarnation, and sacraments in general. He moves on to baptism in chapters 58–65, confirmation in the following chapter, and in chapters 67–8, the Eucharist. It is as if he were moving carefully along an awkward road, watching the condition of the track, and determined to reach his destination by covering every flank![5] His discussion of sacraments links closely with what he said at the beginning of *Laws I*, for he states, 'participation is that mutual inward hold which Christ hath of us and we of him'.[6]

How does this 'participation and conjunction' operate in baptism? Perhaps Hooker answers this question in the following words much later on: 'whether we preach, pray, baptize, communicate, condemn, give absolution, or whatsoever, as disposers of God's mysteries, our words, judgements, acts and deeds are not ours but the Holy Ghost's.'[7] Baptism in Hooker has been little discussed, because much of the attention of various writers and commentators has been taken up either with the general principles with which the book opens, or with the section on the Eucharist and ministry.[8] Moreover, the way Hooker approaches, arranges and discusses his material on baptism is an object-lesson in method. The topics covered in these chapters can be identified as follows:

Chapter 58: the meaning of baptism, its objective character, and the concluding reference to 'things accessory'.

Chapter 59: a discussion of John 3:5 in relation to baptism.

Chapter 60: the necessity of baptism and its availability for all.

Chapter 61: no scriptural evidence for set times or set places for baptism.

Chapter 62: baptism by women – a thorny issue because practised in some places by midwives.

Chapter 63: the profession of Christian faith at baptism.

Chapter 64: the questions to godparents.

Chapter 65: the sign of the cross.

Chapter 66: confirmation.

John Booty believes that *Laws V* was originally drafted as a much shorter book, to which was added, at the instigation of Edwin Sandys and George Cranmer, more contentious material to answer specifically the objections in the Puritan *Admonitions to Parliament*. On his reckoning, the only part which belongs to the original draft on baptism is Chapter 58.[9]

Booty's theory is based on stylistic grounds and it makes a great deal of sense. For example, if we apply his theory to Hooker's discussion of the Eucharist, chapter 67 is a discussion of eucharistic theology, which could indeed stand on its own, whereas chapter 68 – which Booty makes part of the additions to the book – deals with specific Puritan objections, for example, the words of distribution for each communicant, kneeling, and debarring from communion. If this view is correct, then we can expect that chapter 58 can also stand on its own in irenic splendour apart from the remaining chapters, which deal with disputed areas in as polemical a style as Hooker could manage. Let us look at each chapter on baptism in turn, starting with the one which may have been intended to say it all.

In chapter 58, Hooker discusses the relationship between the outward and the inward from two points of view. 'Grace intended by sacraments was a cause of the choice, and there is a reason for the fitness of the elements themselves'.[10] In other words water is used at baptism because of water's properties in creating and sustaining life. (We shall come across this anthropological approach in other writers.) Secondly, he asserts that a sacrament needs three features: the grace which is offered, the element which signifies that grace, and the word which expresses what is done by the element. We are far from Perkins' view of sacrament as a 'prop to faith' and well into a world where sacraments retain their objectivity. Moreover, he trusts what he refers to as 'the known intent of the church generally' to say what baptism is. And he recognizes that in the baptism liturgy there are certain matters which are 'but things accessory, which the wisdom of the church of Christ is to order according to the exigence of that which is principal'.[11]

That is the point at which the discussion might end. If Booty is correct, all that follows was added by Hooker under pressure from his friends, in order to answer controversial matters in a specific sequence and in a sharper style.

The beginning of chapter 59 marks a change of gear, for it sets out to answer those who would deny the *necessity* of baptism. Here, Hooker relies on the words of Jesus to Nicodemus, that no-one can enter the Kingdom of Heaven without being born again of water and the Spirit (John 3:5). Not all Hooker's contemporaries agreed with the medieval Catholic view of the absolute necessity of baptism. His championing of the text from St John that to be thus born again is a consequence of baptism certainly set him apart from Puritans like Cartwright and Perkins. He ends this chapter with a characteristically pithy assertion:

> If on us he accomplish likewise the heavenly work of our new birth not with the Spirit alone but with water thereunto adjoined, sith [since] the faithfullest expanders of words are his own deeds, let that which his hand has manifestly wrought declare what his speech did doubtfully utter.[12]

Chapter 60 carries on the discussion of the necessity of baptism and insists on the unity of the inward and outward, at some variance with Perkins:

> And, if regeneration were not in this very sense a thing necessary to eternal life, would Christ himself talk to Nicodemus that to see the Kingdom of God is impossible, saving only for those men which are born from above?[13]

> ... baptism is a sacrament which God hath instituted in his church, to the end that they which receive the same may thereby be incorporated into Christ, and so through his most precious merit obtain as well that saving grace of imputation which taketh away all former guiltiness, as also

that infused divine virtue of the Holy Ghost, which giveth
to the powers of the soul their first disposition towards
future newness of life.[14]

The inward and outward meet in the sacrament, but the
element of human response is not denied at all. The work of
Christ *imputes* righteousness to the faithful believer, but there
is also an *infused* righteousness which enables human beings
to stand before God as redeemed, and therefore able to worship and serve him.[15] Hooker's understanding of grace is more
traditional than the more severe view of the Puritans. It is all
of a piece with participating in the life of God.

Hooker does not believe that infants who die unbaptized
are damned, because 'grace is not absolutely tied unto the
sacraments'.[16] On the other hand, he is against the Church
'through her superfluous scrupulosity' placing 'lets and
impediments of less regard' in the way of those who want to
be baptized; 'baptism therefore even in the meaning of the
law of Christ belongeth unto infants capable thereof from
the very instant of the birth'.[17]

Chapter 61 concerns set times and places for baptism.
Hooker finds no New Testament evidence for either but he
knows that in the Patristic period Easter and Pentecost were
often set aside for this. He does find evidence for private
baptism, and in so doing clearly has in mind those who are
prepared to turn people away from baptism in order to assert
the public character of the celebration. Hooker's tone at this
point is less than sublime: 'Oh Sir, you that would spurn thus
at such as in case of so dreadful an extremity should lie
prostrate before your feet, you that would turn away your
face from them at the hour of their most need . . .'[18] Many
Puritans would not approve of what would be called emergency baptism.

Chapter 62 tackles the thorny issue of baptism by women,
midwives. This leads on logically from private baptism, par-

ticularly in an age that knew high infant mortality. Many of the Puritans regarded baptism by a midwife as no sacrament at all but an ordinary washing, which meant that the infant should be baptized again. Hooker, to the contrary, finds ancient evidence for such baptisms, and he goes on to assert that 'they that iterate baptism are driven under some pretence or other to make the former baptism void'.[19] This enables Hooker to emphasize yet again the objective nature of baptism: 'baptism is an action in part moral, and in part ecclesiastical, and in part mystical; moral, as being a duty which men perform towards God; ecclesiastical, in that it belongeth to God's church as a public duty; finally mystical, if we respect what God thereby intend to work.'[20] Hooker's overall approach to theology is apparent here. Baptism is moral: it is about lifestyle. Baptism is ecclesiastical: it takes the form of a church liturgy. Baptism is mystical: it brings us into the life of God himself. These three aspects are not separate: they are inextricably bound together, as nature becomes the sacramental vehicle of God's grace in the lives of Christ's disciples.

This discussion leads him to distinguish between those who are old enough to answer for themselves, and infants. Here he uses for the first time the covenant language which Perkins used more fundamentally, and which we shall meet later on in the writings of Baxter, Taylor, Patrick and Thorndike. 'The fruit of baptism dependeth only upon the covenant which God hath made; that God by covenant requireth in the elder sort faith in baptism, in children the sacrament of baptism alone . . . that infants therefore, which have received baptism complete as touching the mystical perfection thereof are by virtue of his own covenant and promise cleansed from all sin . . .'[21] He sums this up in a glorious nugget: 'the grace of baptism cometh by donation of God alone.'[22]

Chapter 63 deals with a corollary of infant baptism, the profession of Christian faith by godparents. Here, Hooker is firmly traditional. 'The first thing required of him that standeth for admission into Christ's family is belief. Which belief consisteth not so much in knowledge as in acknowledgement of all things that heavenly wisdom revealeth; the affection of faith is above her reach, her love to Godward above the comprehension of God.'[23] He expresses the nature of this profession by quoting the sixth-century writer Isidore of Seville, who spells out in covenant terms the renunciation of evil and profession of Christian faith. 'Two covenants there are which Christian men do make in baptism, the one concerning relinquishment of Satan, the other touching obedience to the faith of God.' (Covenant imagery was known among the Fathers, and was not just a biblical motif that lay dormant until the Reformation.) And he goes on to say, 'neither do I think it a matter easy for any man to prove, that ever baptism did use to be administered without interrogatories of these two kinds.'[24]

Chapter 64 concerns the use of godparents themselves. Many Puritans probably ignored this ingredient in the baptism service altogether, and asked the parents to make the profession of faith on behalf of their own child. But as if to secure common ground, Hooker states at the outset, 'they with whom we contend are no enemies to the baptism of infants'.[25] Once again he uses covenant language. As we have already seen, Hooker knew that it was used by Isidore of Seville. But he would also have been fully aware of its popularity among the new Puritans. We may conclude that this was part of his intention, to try to get them on his side.

> . . . baptism implieth a covenant or league between God and man, wherein as God and man, wherein as God doth bestow presently remission of sins and the Holy Ghost, binding all to himself to add in process of time what grace soever shall be further necessary for the attainment of everlasting life . . .

and:

> The law of Christ requiring therefore faith and newness of life in all men by virtue of the covenant which they make in baptism, is it toyish that the church in baptism exacteth at every man's hands an express profession of faith and an irrevocable promise of obedience by way of solemn stipulation?

and:

> That infants may contract and covenant with God, the law is plain.[26]

('Toyish' was used in the *First Admonition to Parliament*, and by Cartwright, of this very matter.) Hooker was at this point arguing for godparents, not to deflect responsibility from parents, but in order to encompass the whole Church presenting the child for baptism, and to place further emphasis on the potential spiritual growth of the child. If children are in the covenant of grace under God, then there can be no question that godparents are inappropriate as sponsors in that future growth. Again and again in Hooker's approach to baptism we see the motif of God's future, as we live and grow in his grace.

Chapter 65 is a lengthy discussion about the sign of the cross. As the only remaining sign of the cross still directed in the Prayer Book after the Reformation it will have stood out a mile to those who found it a dumb ceremony reminiscent of the medieval Catholic inheritance. Puritan clergy may well have omitted it, perhaps adapting the Prayer Book formula about fighting with the banner of Christ that accompanied it in the process. The fact that the signing of the cross had been given before baptism in the medieval rite, and that Lutherans retained it there, may well have contributed to an atmosphere of debate.[27] But for Hooker it was a test case in how to argue for tradition not on the grounds of what has been done in the past but because of intrinsic meaning. 'Lest therefore the name of tradition should be offensive to any, considering how far by some it hath been and is abused, we mean by traditions, ordinances made in the prime of Christian religion . . .'[28]

Hooker continues in a psychological vein: 'ceremonies have more in weight than in sight, they work by commonness of use much, although in the several acts of their usage we scarcely discern any good they do.' And specifically of the cross: 'for prevention whereof when we use this ceremony we always plainly express the end whereunto it serveth, namely, for a sign of remembrance'.[29] In other words, Hooker knows that the sign of the cross goes back far into antiquity, it has a psychological impact that does not require its own defence, and it is a remembrance at the profoundest level of the central sign of the Christian faith. The notion of memory Hooker will have known from Augustine's *Confessions*.[30] He is clearly captivated by it in relation to the cross, for he mentions it no fewer than six times. The first time he asserts: 'surely the wisdom of the Church of Christ which hath to that use converted the ceremony of the cross in baptism it is no Christian man's part to despise, especially seeing that by this mean where nature doth earnestly implore aid, religion yieldeth her that ready assistance than which there can be no help more forcible serving only to relieve memory, and to bring to our cogitation that which should most make ashamed of sin.' On successive occasions he goes on to refer to the cross as 'the memory of that sign', 'memorials of duty', 'that special note of remembrance', and 'that ceremony of the cross which serveth only for a sign of remembrance'.[31] And he ends firmly, 'touching therefore the sign and ceremony of the cross, we no-way find ourselves bound to relinquish it'.[32]

Chapter 66 covers the question of confirmation. Like Perkins, Hooker knows that the laying on of hands by the bishop was given in antiquity on many different kinds of occasion. 'With prayers of spiritual and personal benediction the manner hath been in all ages to use imposition of hands as a ceremony betokening our restrained desires to the party, whom we present unto God by prayer.'[33] But he concludes, unlike Perkins, that the Fathers held confirmation to be apostolic, which is difficult to support. He understands that baptism was severed from confirmation, which it certainly was, and that the laying on of hands was used for receiving back heretics. Hooker falls for the temptation to view confirmation by a bishop as pertaining to 'the dignity of her superiors'. But he states that 'confirmation is only a sacramental complement'.[34] Confirmation is worthwhile. It is not a sacrament. It is not better than baptism simply because it is conferred by a bishop, and it gives strength against temptation.

What are we to make of Hooker on baptism? In his work of Book V of *The Laws*, Francis Paget lists the printings of the whole, from the very first, through the various seventeenth-century editions, and continuing after 1665, ending in the nineteenth century with those of Dobson, Hanbury, and (most importantly) Keble.[35] The Folger Library edition of all Hooker's works, with its commentaries, represents the summation of Hooker scholarship to date. From all this, it can be seen that Hooker has had a fuller airing and influence in the past two centuries than Perkins, whose complete works by contrast have known no full publication since the first part of the seventeenth century.

As to Hooker's method, we have witnessed his obvious talent not only at explaining but at justifying. Indeed, it is interesting to note the cross-references and citations to Thomas Cartwright's *Replies* to Whitgift's *Answers* to the *Admonitions to Parliament* which appear in his footnotes. Not one occurs in chapter 58, but there are over thirty spread across the ensuing chapters, a further corroboration of

Booty's suggestion that 58 was originally written as complete in itself, and that the remaining discussion was added in order to deal with controversial matters in a bolder fashion.[36]

Assuredly, Hooker builds a solid edifice in which tradition is placed under scrutiny but remains broadly intact. For Hooker, baptism is primarily the means of drawing us into participation in the life of God. The believer is able to share in that life through fellowship with God, is able to abide in that life through Christ indwelling, and is able again and again to return to God through that repentance which lies at the heart of the baptismal relationship with God. This may explain why original sin, and sin in general, is not mentioned in Hooker's discussion, whereas it is by Perkins. From his opening chapter, which reads clearly and sublimely, he moves on into more controversial terrain, insisting on the unity of the inward and the outward, and the necessity of baptism for all (even though some of his contemporaries, including Archbishop Whitgift, were not at one with him here). Baptism is for all. Midwives must be allowed to baptize in emergencies. The renunciation of evil and profession of faith in Christ express that baptismal life and are part of the way in which we relate to Christ in a living sense. Godparents lead infants towards a growing faith on behalf of the whole community, for baptism is not just about families. The sign of the cross is a living memory of the central act of salvation. Confirmation by the bishop through the laying on of hands is the next stage in Christian nurture.

He sees the danger of divorcing the inward and the outward, which he will have known from his reading of Perkins, even though Perkins does not receive one single mention in his somewhat select footnotes. His pastoral heart and love of tradition ensure that private baptism – firmly embedded in the Prayer Book as a liturgy in its own right – should not be superseded by select public occasions.

He draws us again and again to the font, where we begin

our journey into the life of God. Indeed, his whole under-standing of sacraments is that they are in fact one, a means of living in Christ; and both in this, and in his 'instrumental' view of the working of the sacrament, he emerges with what might be called 'High Calvinist' leanings. However, like many of the other divines, he does not follow Calvin in rejecting those traditional liturgical and pastoral practices associated with baptism for centuries which made so much theological sense to him. As Olivier Loyer succinctly puts it in his study of Hooker's theology: 'there is in fact only one sacrament; for every sacrament makes us participants in the body of Christ. This is why Hooker insists with such force on the unity of baptism and eucharist ... baptism throws the first divine seed into our soul; it grafts us into the mystical body.'[37] Baptism indeed 'throws the first divine seed into our soul' and for Hooker that seed simply cannot fail to grow, even though we ourselves may not be aware of it much of the time.

5

Heaven Opened

Lancelot Andrewes (1555–1626)

I well remember the first time that I presided at a public baptism. It was in the summer of 1974, when a large extended family gathered around the medieval font near the back of the imposing parish church of St Wulfram in Grantham. The octagonal font is placed on steps because of the size of the building. Scenes from the life of Christ are carved into the stonework against the bowl, and these include the baptism of Christ, which figures – in one way or another – in each of the four Gospels.

St Wulfram's had a wide interior dating from the late thirteenth and fourteenth centuries. As if to draw yet more attention to the font, a very tall font cover was placed over it in 1899, designed by Sir Walter Tapper. It is so large that unlike other covers of its kind it does not lift off through a pulley mechanism; instead, there are two doors in the side which open out. Any person baptized is therefore taken into darkness before water is poured over their head! Covering fonts in this way is a time-honoured device to preserve holy water from those who would misuse it, and to add reverence to the sacramental function of the font.

The combination of the position of this font near the rear of the church and doors in the font cover which provide access to the baptismal water only serves to underline an important biblical image which brings us to the heart of the mystery of baptism. For the Bible is full of doors and gates. Jesus is the door of the sheep (John 10:9), yet the doors were shut when the disciples gathered together in the upper room after Jesus' death (John 20:19). In Matthew and Mark the stone is rolled against the door to Christ's tomb (Matt. 27:60, Mark 15:46), through which Christ's resurrection manages to break free.

Most notably of all, there are gateways and doors in that most tantalizing of New Testament books, the Revelation to St John. The new Jerusalem has twelve gates, carefully described (Rev. 21:12 ff.). The church in Philadelphia has an open door set before it, which no-one has been able to shut (Rev. 3:8). The Lord stands at the door and knocks, and if anyone hears his voice and opens the door, he will come to him and eat with him, for the church in Laodicea (Rev. 3:20). After these two concluding letters in the series to the seven churches in Asia, the following chapter opens with the words, 'After this I looked, and lo, in heaven an open door!' (Rev. 4:1). All this suggests, too, the words of Jacob when he awoke from dreaming of a ladder between earth and heaven, and angels ascending and descending: 'How awesome is this place! This is none other than the house of God, and this is the gate of heaven' (Gen. 28:17).

But how does the image of the door relate to baptism? The first way is that baptism is about the future. In all the accounts of Christ's baptism, it is clear from what follows that baptism was an important stage in starting Jesus off on his ministry. In Matthew, Mark and Luke, Jesus goes straight into the wilderness (Matt. 3:13 ff., Mark 1:9 ff., Luke 3:21 ff.), but, interestingly, Luke places the genealogy of Jesus back to Adam between the baptism and the temptation in the wilderness. Baptism, therefore, can be seen as a beginning and not as a result. Many discussions about baptism 'policy' at the local level fail to take into account that baptism is primarily an act of God and a focus for his grace in the future. In Jesus' case, in the three accounts just quoted, the great moment of baptism leads Jesus into the wilderness, where he wrestles with his vocation, after which his ministry begins. He did not have to 'qualify' for God's anointing Spirit. The anointing Spirit was given freely.

Secondly, baptism is a moment in time and eternity when God's love and forgiveness are celebrated and given. To place the font near a church door is to suggest that we are baptised on entry and then go forward to the chancel steps for confirmation and thereafter to the altar for communion. Baptism is the gate of heaven, the door to newness of life. Baptism *is* the open door. And when that door is open in *heaven*, past, present and future exist as a single whole.[1] One is reminded of the words from the Prayer Book baptism service quoted earlier: 'so give now unto us that ask; let us that seek find; open the gate unto us that knock; that this infant may enjoy the everlasting benediction of thy heavenly washing, and may come to the eternal kingdom which thou hast promised by Christ our Lord.'[2]

Thirdly, the door suggests opportunity. Every time we stroll past the font, physically or mentally, we are given a visual expression of the new beginning that Christ will always offer to those who come to him. The new beginning is about repentance and renewal, not in abstract ways but in the concrete reality of our ordinary lives. When I preside at baptism and confirmation as a bishop, I often insert a brief reference to the Bible readings before the renunciation and the profession of faith. This is my way of suggesting that they are going to go on and on renouncing the devil and professing faith in Christ in countless ways all through their lives. Baptism opens a door and keeps that door open. Or to revert to the death and resurrection of Christ, we can roll the stone against the door of the tomb, and shut the doors against the world, but Christ keeps coming to burst out of the tomb and to make his entrance into our fearful lives.

*   *   *

'Heaven opened' could well be the title of the sermon on the baptism of Christ preached by Bishop Lancelot Andrewes before the Court of King James I at Whitsun, on Sunday 29 May 1615.[3]

By 1615, Andrewes was a substantial figure in the realm. When he died in 1626, ninety-six of his sermons were edited, collected together and published in 1629 at the direction of King Charles I. He had preached all through his ministry, going back to the time when he was Catechist to Pembroke Hall, Cambridge. He was then Vicar at St Giles' in Cripplegate, London, and from 1601 until 1605 Dean of Westminster, but it was as a Bishop that his sermons were perhaps best known. The ninety-six that were published include seventeen for Christmas Day, preached between 1605 and 1624; eighteen for Easter Day, preached between 1606 and 1623 with an additional one prepared but not actually delivered because of declining health; and fourteen preached on Whitsunday, with an additional fifteenth again prepared for delivery, in 1622, but again not delivered because of ill health. Each one of the Christmas sermons was preached at Whitehall. Nearly all the Easter Day sermons were also preached at Whitehall, with the exception of the twelfth, preached in Durham Cathedral in 1617, as the Court progressed north to Edinburgh for the fiftieth anniversary of the coronation of King James as King of Scotland. The Whitsun sermons, however, are divided between Greenwich (mostly) and Whitehall, with one at Windsor and the 1617 preachment at Holyrood for that special anniversary of the King.

As a sixty-year-old senior diocesan in 1615, Andrewes was at the height of his influence. Four years later he was to become Bishop of Winchester, but most of these 'royal sermons' were preached during his ten years as Bishop of Ely. The Royal Chapel at Greenwich was probably quite a small building, seating about 40–60 people. One can imagine an interior with boxed pews on either side of the nave, special pews, perhaps facing opposite the pulpit, for the King and the immediate royal entourage, and an altar against the east end, doubtless railed off for communicants to kneel. There would almost certainly have been a font, and if Andrewes or any of his immediate colleagues had had a hand in the furnishings of the chapel, the font would have been placed near the door, or else somewhere near the small area in front of the pulpit at the head of the nave. King James liked a good sermon, was keen on theological argument, and would without doubt have seen that his position in chapel was prominent, affording a good view of the preacher, especially if the preacher were Andrewes, his favoured homilist at festivals.

Andrewes' Whitsun sermons are probably among his most outstanding.[4] Like the other festival preachings, they form a unity in themselves. Indeed, one senses that the Whitsun sermons were particularly dear to the preacher's heart, given his vivid understanding of the work of the Holy Spirit. The texts that he uses are frequently from the Acts of the Apostles, or John's Gospel, or, on one occasion, the First Epistle of St John. On only two occasions does he take his text from Luke's Gospel, in Holyrood in 1617 (Luke 4:18–19, 'The Spirit of the Lord is upon me . . .'[5]) and for the 1615 sermon. For this occasion he chooses Luke's narrative of the baptism of Christ (Luke 3:22–2) and it is important to see why he may have deliberately chosen this particular narrative. A brief comparison may be useful.

In Matthew's version (Matt. 3:13–17) Jesus goes from Galilee to the River Jordan and tells John that he needs to be baptized. John challenges him; he is baptized nonetheless; heaven is opened and the Spirit comes like a dove; and the voice says: '*This* is my beloved . . .' In Mark's Gospel (Mark 1:9–12), Jesus comes from Nazareth; there is no dialogue with John beforehand; he is baptized, heaven is opened; the Spirit comes like a dove; but the voice addresses Jesus directly: '*Thou art my beloved son . . .*' Luke's narrative, however, has some notable differences. *All* the people are being baptized, and Jesus is then baptized; and he then *prays*, whereupon heaven opens and the Spirit appears *in bodily form* as a dove; and the voice addresses Jesus directly: 'Thou art my beloved son'. In other words, all the people are there with Jesus; Jesus prays; the Spirit appears in bodily form; and there is the Marcan direct speech. Each one of these features is brought out in Andrewes' sermon. To that we must now turn.

'This is the feast of the Holy Ghost. And here we have in the text, a visible descending of the Holy Ghost.'[6] That single sentence, forming one paragraph, is an eloquent statement of Andrewes' theology of Whitsun – and baptism. He compares the lesson which will have been read in the course of the Eucharist (Acts 2:1–11), on which he preached on the first two occasions, which were also at Greenwich. But the Lucan narrative 'hath the vantage of it', because it tells of Christ's *baptism*, which was the first descending of the Holy Spirit, and – significantly – because whereas the Acts reading tells us of the making of the Apostles into Christians, Christ's baptism is about *all of us* becoming Christians. Andrewes is not an exclusive preacher.

Moreover, he goes on to describe Whitsun as 'the Feast of Baptism', for the event is dramatic: '. . . by the opening of heaven . . . For here is the whole Trinity in person. The Son in the water, the Holy Ghost in the dove, the Father in the voice.'[7] To bring the Trinity into the beginning of a sermon is one of Andrewes' devices. In the 1612 Whitsun sermon he declares in a similar vein, 'the Father in the voice, the Son in the flood, the Holy Ghost in the shape of a dove'.[8] The only other time, Andrewes points out, when the Trinity appears in the Bible is in the Old Testament at the beginning of creation: 'there we find God, and the word with God creating, and the Spirit of God moving upon the face of the waters.

And now here again at Christ's christening in the new.'[9] That was at the creation, now we have a *new* creation.[10]

Andrewes wants to involve the people at every stage, for in the Lucan narrative Jesus is baptized along with the people. By a neat device, he draws their own baptism at the hands of John the Baptist into Christ's baptism by referring to its being 'not only for their sin; even their righteousness (take it at the best), even that, was not so clean, but it needs baptism'.[11] And with a rich assemblage of Old Testament texts on washing the unclean, Andrewes asserts – with what would nowadays be called an anthropological touch – that we need not only need the baptism of the *womb* but the baptism of the *laver of regeneration*.

We now move to the baptism of Christ himself. He was baptized with the people, to show that he was an example, 'a good example of humility, as he did at his Maundy, when he washed his disciples' feet'.[12] And as if to cast a mild slur on private individual baptisms, he says: 'and when? not upon a day by himself, but when they. And where? Not in a basin by himself but even in the common river, with the rest of the meiny [household].'[13] No doubt Andrewes was thinking of the Royal Court as a household, by now a familiar group to him.

Christ stands there on our behalf, acting 'as having two capacities . . . as a person of himself, and as the author of a race or head of a society'. Our solidarity with Christ is collective, not individual. In alluding to blessing the water in the baptismal liturgy, Andrewes uses a well-known motif from the Fathers: 'Jordan had no more need to come to him, than he to Jordan, to be cleansed . . . he received no cleanness, no virtue; but virtue he gave, to Jordan, to the waters, to the sacrament itself.'[14] Such is the identification between Christ and the human race, 'that in his baptism he puts us on; as we put him on, in ours'. It will be remembered how important a text Galatians 3:27 was for Perkins' baptismal theology.[15]

At this stage, Andrewes spreads his net widely and refers to a three-fold immersion which is not counted in scripture but is – yet again – in the liturgy. He identifies these immersions as the immersion in Gethsemane during Christ's agony, the immersion at Gabbatha when he was scourged, and the third at Golgotha at the Crucifixion. In the last, 'there met the two streams of water and blood, the true Jordan, the bath of laver wherein we are purged from all our sins . . . And therefore are we baptized into it; not into his water-baptism, but into his cross-baptism . . .' It is hard not to see in this passage a powerful implied reference to the sign of the cross at baptism – which he had, after all, defended before King James, in front of the Puritans, at the Hampton Court conference in 1604.[16]

This leads Andrewes to insist on the need for baptism; 'for, if when the people was baptized, Christ was so: much more strongly it holds; when Christ himself is so, that then, the people should and ought to be baptized'.[17] Christ now prays. 'Want begets prayer: therefore, yet there wants somewhat. A part, and that a chief part of baptism, is still behind.' For the baptism is not just of water, it is blood and the Spirit, the power of God, and he refers again to the three immersions, thinking of the liturgy still. For Andrewes, baptism is more than an outward sign, it is an inward reality, an action of God in the orbit of human lives.

Baptism is a giving of the Holy Spirit, as Christ states to Nicodemus (John 3:5). Andrewes draws together the inward and the outward aspects of baptism, for when Paul talks about baptism in the water and the cloud (I Cor. 10:2), Andrewes speaks of 'the baptism of the body' and 'the baptism of the soul'. There can be no theological difference between baptism of the water and baptism of the Spirit, for – in words reminiscent of Hooker – 'in baptism, besides the hand seen, that casts in the water: the virtue of the Holy Ghost is there, working, without hands, what here was wrought.'[18]

Christ's prayer is for all people who will be baptized after him. 'See the force of his prayer. Before it, heaven was mured up, no dove to be seen, no voice to be heard . . . but straight upon it (as if they had but waited the last word of his prayer) all of them followed immediately.' He goes on: 'the prayer of Christ shall it not be much more a force, to enter the heaven of heavens, the highest of them all, and to bring down thence the waters above the heavens, even the heavenly grace of the Holy Spirit'; and: 'always, the opening of heaven, opens unto us, that no baptism without heaven, open . . . for heavengate . . . doth ever open at baptism.'[19] Here we have Andrewes' theology of baptism in a nutshell.

The Holy Spirit comes down upon Christ 'not to make him to be ought; but to show him only, to be'.[20] He comes, in other words, permanently on Christ, showing him to be the Son of God, as the Spirit descends permanently on us at our baptism to adopt us as God's children. Doves flutter around but this dove fixes upon Christ – as that dove fixes on each one of us at our baptism. The corporate aspect of baptism is stressed again when Andrewes draws attention to the fact that the people who are around Christ at his baptism (according to Luke's version) were able to witness the descent of the dove.

Andrewes now goes into a delightful diversion about differ-ent kinds of dove. I once heard it remarked that these sermons are a little like a Shakespeare play, with different types of characters coming on to the stage and relating in different ways to the basic narrative, and sometimes providing, as do Trinculo and Stephano in *The Tempest*, some entertainment. The dove section has its serious side. There is Noah's dove which is that of peace (Gen. 8:11). There is the Psalmist's dove of silver white, full of virtue (Ps. 68:13). There is Isaiah's dove, with patient murmuring (Isa. 38:14). And then there is the dove which Christ mentions to his disciples as a paradigm of innocence (Matt. 10:16).[21]

This leads him into some overt polemic with the Roman

Catholic Church, which reads somewhat harshly to twen-
tieth-century ears. Andrewes had engaged with two leading
Roman Catholic theologians over the years, first Cardinal
Bellarmine, with his *Responsio* (1610), and then Cardinal
Du Perron, with his *Two Answers*. Now, at a much more
aggressive level, a Jesuit called Thomas Fitzherbert had written against the 'very many foul absurdities, falsities and lies' of
Bishop Andrewes in a work published in 1613.[22] The Roman
Church tried to claim the keys to the Kingdom of Heaven,
but Andrewes now goes so far as to say that a vulture and
not a dove descended on it instead! He contrasts thus: 'the
date of these meek and patient christians is worn out' – referring to the earlier Fathers – and 'the shape of the Roman
eagle' has taken over.[23] But Andrewes, for all that he may
have been stung by this level of controversy, cannot bring
himself to deny the validity of their baptism. 'That shape
came down upon Christ, the same, comes down on us all
that are baptized, with his baptism; and are inspired with the
same Spirit, that he was.'[24] Nevertheless, he shows what might
be described as Anglican detachment in stating 'christians
are made in a cooler element' – away from the heat of
controversy.

The voice of God now speaks at Christ's baptism. The
voice is that of the dove, speaking over the water. He uses
the Augustine tag, 'accedat verbum ad elementum' – 'let the
word be added to the element',[25] which makes it into a 'visible
word'. The work of God in Trinity is once more emphasized,
and we are drawn again into the scene – 'indeed, his whole
baptism is not so much his, as ours.'[26] For we are 'in league
with him, in the new league, (or covenant) never to be altered
. . . so may we be, and stranger still; nay no strangers, but
naturalized, and of the commonwealth of Israel'. We are part
of God's household, fully fledged members, even *'franchised'*,
and like the Father of the Prodigal Son, God is always ready
to welcome us home. 'A son, a beloved son, his father's delight

and joy; there is no degree higher.'[27] 'At first, we were but washed from our sins ... but here, from a baptized sinner, to an adopted son, is a great ascent.' The metaphor of rebirth takes over from that of washing. 'This, the very feast of adoption. A feast therefore, to be held in high account with us; as high as we hold this (to be the adopted children of God).'[28]

Andrewes ends his sermon with another favourite device, relating his text to the Eucharist and the life of heaven.

> To baptism we may not come again ... so out of it to apply to us, another way; as it were in supplement of baptism ... in whom he receiveth so, to his table, to eat and drink with him, ... with them he is well pleased again, certainly. On this day of the Spirit, every benefit of the Spirit, is set forth and offered us; and we shall please him well, in making benefit of all. Specially to this, the only means, to renew his complacency [pleasure], and to restore us thither, where our baptism left us.[29]

Andrewes' sermons are rich fare. They were published in various editions from 1629 onwards and were read by successive generations of clergy and laity, but their popularity diminished as time went on. They were reprinted in 1841 and provide us with a bird's eye view into the mind of one of the most remarkable thinkers and preachers of his age. His was an ecumenism of the Spirit, always able to draw different strands together and address the present with an engaging and challenging originality. He read Richard Hooker and counted him among his many friends. They share many attributes, not least what we would nowadays call a dynamic anthropology, in which human nature is fallen, but redeemed. As he remarks in a sermon on prayer, 'although, Lord, I have lost the duty of a son, yet Thou hast not lost the affection of a father'.[30] The God whom Andrewes preaches never let the human race down.

In this Whitsun sermon, we get a picture of a Trinitarian theology. We are drawn into Christ's baptism inevitably. Among his private prayers, there is a thanksgiving for 'the most sacred baptism, the appearing therein of the Trinity'.[31] Here there is no distinction between the inward and the outward in the sacramental act. Spiritual growth is a necessary consequence of a sacramental life, as witness the way in which Andrewes draws his hearers to contemplate the baptism of Christ and to partake of the Eucharist.

There are important suggestions of liturgical practice. Baptism is with three immersions. No basins or private ceremonies should normally be used, but presumably the large fonts are the old ones. There is such a stress on Christ's solidarity with his people that it is tempting to suggest that in this mutual relationship and promise of future new life are to be found convictions that lay hold on godparents, their renunciation of evil and their profession of faith. Moreover baptism is no mere option, to be taken lightly, but is a sacrament towards which we are all drawn. It is our participation in Christ's life, including the crucifixion – a suggestion, indeed, of the sign of the cross at baptism. Baptism is unrepeatable, because it can stand on its own without any supplement. It is the Eucharist's task to provide sacramentally subsequent feeding and sustenance. Basic to Andrewes' approach, however, is the *narrative* of Christ's baptism as, the means whereby we are made one with him in history and eternity. In this aspect, Andrewes pioneers an important insight in which he is followed by Taylor and Thorndike.

Christ's prayer, Christ's action in going to the Jordan and blessing it and praying for all who will be baptized in the future – all this suggests a liturgical picture. At the very heart of it is the scene of heaven opening. This provides the clue for Andrewes' understanding of the Church, which is essentially a baptismal one. Nicholas Lossky, a Russian Orthodox lay theologian teaching in Paris, has written a detailed study of Andrewes' preaching and relates it to the traditional Eastern view of the bishop-theologian teaching the Christian faith at the festivals. He writes:

> . . . in other respects, the definition of the Church that can be discerned in the preaching of Lancelot Andrewes is essentially positive. Instead of the Church's being defined by its visible and perceptible limits, by relation to those who are outside it, the Church is defined positively, in its essence, as the place where the Spirit of Truth blows who is to be distinguished at once from the 'private spirit' and the 'spirit of the world'.[32]

Andrewes understood the importance of good liturgical practice, and in his Visitation Articles he follows many of his episcopal colleagues in enquiring whether the set order of service is used, including at baptism; whether private baptism is only celebrated when necessary; whether priests refuse baptism when the child is seriously ill; whether the sign of the cross is used as directed in the service; whether baptism is celebrated in the usual font rather than a basin; whether parents act as godparents to their own children; whether the priests catechize children properly and bring them to confirmation; and much else besides.[33] He knew of the historic and primitive practice of anointing at baptism, as it clear from elsewhere in his sermons,[34] but he never proposed it for liturgical use. In other words, Andrewes' preaching and his liturgical discipline were at one with each other, inseparably linked aspects of the same teacher, the same mystagogue.

Andrewes is clearly a man of his times, however contemporary he feels himself to be with witnesses belonging to the past. His constant concern is clearly the coming-to-be of the Church of his own time, the Church being seen not as a global abstraction but as a body composed of members.[35]

So writes Nicholas Lossky, and he surely expresses the almost iconographic quality of Andrewes' approach to the theology of baptism. We are drawn towards Christ, and we continue to be drawn to him, as we stroll past that font, on our walk together through the doors of eternity into heaven itself, and are gathered through his prayers into God's eternal dwelling-place.[36]

6

Providence

George Herbert (1593–1633)

I have been present at countless discussions of baptism. Indeed, when I was listening to the General Synod of the Church of England debating proposed new services for baptism at the end of November, 1996, I started having a strange sense of history repeating itself. The same issues came up again and again. One particular question focused on the promises at baptism; should the godparents promise on behalf of the child, or for themselves as well as on behalf of the child? The Prayer Book opts for the former, but the 1980 *Alternative Service Book* opts for the latter, in common with other modern rites today.

At the heart of the discussion, there are two foundation-points in the nature of baptism. On the one hand, baptism cannot be repeated. On the other hand, because it is unrepeatable, we have to trust in the providence of God. Such an understanding of baptism has pastoral and human consequences. Those who want to hedge around baptism with the 'lets and impediments' of Richard Hooker[1] may well be cautious about the use of godparents and see the children of *believing* parents as already in the covenant and therefore eligible for baptism.

Such an approach has a great deal to commend it. It is consistent. It places a great deal of emphasis on the unrepeatability of baptism. It may well rely, too, on the kind of distinction between the inward and the outward baptism which we saw in the writings of William Perkins.[2] But as we have already seen, the balance between the unrepeatable character of baptism and trust in the providence of God enabled another view to grow which has a great deal of tradition behind it. Controversy can often be the sign of the health of a Christian community, particularly if the controversy goes to the heart of the real issues rather than remaining in the periphery.

One of the speeches in that General Synod debate ended on a point of caution about these 'lets and impediments', declaring that in the celebration of Christian baptism we are dealing with the paradox of the love of God, who is both affection and demand, both mystery and accessibility. These tensions run right through so much: a Christian gospel which is all affection and no demand is flabby, whereas one which is all demand and no affection is exclusive. Similarly, a God who is all mystery and no accessibility may be deeply religious, but cuts no ice with the world as we know it; and a God who is all accessibility can easily become the creation of the latest trend.

We are particularly prone in a decade of self-styled 'evangelism' to bring into our Christian parlance and attitudes some of the less attractive attitudes of the world we live in. This has always been the case. The culture of self-determination today is indeed one of these. According to that fashion, we must decide everything for ourselves, we must be free to choose, we become God's customers rather than his subjects, which gives us rights, rather than privileges or duties.

The culture of self-determination sits uncomfortably with the Christian tradition. One of the most powerful statements of this kind that was ever written is the *Confessions* of St Augustine.[3] Augustine was no indiscriminate baptizer, for to him baptism was a momentous part of his own journey through the religions and philosophies available to him in a civilization where they were all very much in the market place. Indeed, there is an almost deliberately stark simplicity about a sentence which is tucked away in Book 9 of the *Confessions*: 'We were baptized, and disquiet about our past life vanished from us.'[4] Right through Augustine's preaching career, Easter baptism held a central and powerful place.[5] For Augustine his baptism was part of God's plan for him; and that little sentence needs to be seen – for doubtless Augustine intended it so – in the much wider context of a book, a life, which kept probing and exploring human experience for meaning, stability and coherence. After all, this is how the *Confessions* starts: 'You stir man to take pleasure in praising you, because you have made us for yourself, and our heart is restless until it rests in you.'[6] The *Confessions* was read by priests and theologians on all sides of the Reformation conflicts of the sixteenth and seventeenth centuries. There is much that one can take from the *Confessions* but its key principle is God's prevenient grace, the belief that God walks ahead of us and that his promises will not fail.[7] Although providence and the prevenient grace of God figure in many other writings of the period we are looking at, they are particularly prominent in the works of the priest-poet George Herbert.[8]

A difficulty with George Herbert is that he is a legend. This is partly because Izaak Walton wrote a flattering biography.[9] The other reason is that Herbert's poetry became popular among all sections of religious opinion through the seventeenth century. Like Andrewes, he has experienced something of a comeback this century, and this is in no small measure due to T. S. Eliot's devotion to him. Part of the false legend sees Herbert as a sublime figure, but as Eliot himself points out, 'to think of Herbert as the poet of a placid and comfortable easy piety is to misunderstand utterly the man and his poems'.[10]

But poet he certainly was. Of Welsh aristocratic stock, he

had a distinguished career at Cambridge and was Public Orator at Cambridge before he was even twenty-seven – an honour which would have led others to expect high office. For some reason that is not altogether clear, he forsook high life and became Rector of Leighton Bromswold in 1626. Four years later – at Archbishop Laud's behest – he became Rector of Bemerton, near Salisbury, and Sub-Dean of the Cathedral, following in the footsteps of Hooker. While at Leighton Bromswold, he became a close friend of Nicholas Ferrar, who had set up an informal mixed religious community at Little Gidding. The interior of Leighton Bromswold Church owes something to Herbert's dedication; inside were placed at identical levels on the floor a pair of matching canopied ambos to serve as pulpit and reading desk.[11] Such dual pulpit/reading desks were not uncommon in the seventeenth century, and were regarded as the hallmark of those who wanted to give architectural expression to the Prayer Book liturgical principle that preaching and prayer were on an equal footing in worship and piety.

It was during his years at Bemerton that Herbert was able to complete his two major works, *The Priest to the Temple* (1632) and *The Temple* (1633). He had written poems virtually all his life and there are some Latin poems from an earlier time that we shall also be looking at. But it is worth pausing in order to note that Herbert stands out from among the writers we have looked at so far, and indeed from those that we shall be looking at later, in that he was a *poet*. Although his poetry was published and republished in subsequent centuries, they circulated only among his friends during his lifetime. Thus we have the picture of a very private man, whose life is not without its paradoxes: Public Orator at Cambridge, humble country parson in Wiltshire. Moreover, unlike some of his contemporaries, such as John Donne, Herbert's prose and poetic style is simple and direct. There is an integrity between Herbert's expressed ideals for the parson and the poems in *The Temple*, as well as in the polemical Latin poems that he wrote earlier. To these we must now turn.

Although Herbert completed *A Priest to the Temple* in 1632, it was not published until 1652. It comes in thirty-seven short chapters, each approximately the same length, namely a lengthy paragraph. As Stanley Stewart has stated, 'George Herbert wrote one of the few handbooks for priests published during the 17th century.'[12] The style certainly suggests the 'handbook's' intention. Chapter one gives a definition of the parson; chapter two deals with 'Their Diversities'; chapter three with the parson's life; four, the parson's knowledge; five, the parson's accessory knowledge (recognizing that priests needn't know everything!). Chapter six is about the parson praying, which is followed in chapter seven by the parson preaching. Note carefully the order: here in literary and theological form is the outworking of the twin pulpit/reading desk in Leighton Bromswold Church, the prayer before the sermon. Subsequent chapters deal with lifestyle, home life, courtesy, charity, the care of the inside of the Church, and then pastoral work – comforting and visiting, and as a point of reference in the community. Only at chapter twenty-one do we come across the parson catechizing; it is as if in Herbert's view the work of the priest should be as wide as possible in its starting point, before being narrowly focused on what happens in church.

Chapter twenty-two deals with the parson in the sacraments.[13] Here is the first part, on baptism.

The County Parson being to administer the Sacraments, is at a stand with himself, how or what behaviour to assume for so holy things. Especially at Communion time he is in a great confusion, as being not only to receive God, but to break, and administer him. Neither finds he any issue in this, but to throw himself down at the throne of grace, saying, Lord, thou knowest what thou didst, when thou appointedst it to be done thus; therefore do thou fulfil what Thou didst appoint; for thou art not only the feast, but the way to it. At Baptism, being himself in white, he requires the presence of all, and baptizeth not willingly, but [except] on Sundays, or great days. He admits no vain or idle names, but such as are usual and accustomed. He says that prayer with great devotion, where God is thanked for calling us to the knowledge of his grace, Baptism being a blessing, that the world hath not the like. He willingly and cheerfully crosseth the child, and thinketh the ceremony not only innocent, but reverend. He instructeth the Godfathers and Godmothers, that it is no complemental or light thing to sustain that place, but a great honour, and no less burden, as being done both in the presence of God, and his Saints, and by way of undertaking for a Christian soul. He adviseth all to call to mind their Baptism often: for if wise men have thought it the best way of preserving a state to reduce it to its principles by which it grew great; certainly, it is the safest course for Christians also to meditate on their Baptism often (being the first step into their great and glorious calling) and upon what terms, and with what vows they were baptized.

A great deal can be gleaned from this passage. The parson must approach the sacraments with a sense of awe, throwing himself at the mercy of God. Here we have the same sense of reverence that we came across in Richard Hooker. In what Herbert has to say specifically about baptism, there are no fewer than seven important truths.

First, the parson is dressed in white – the white surplice. Perhaps there were some who did not bother to wear a surplice for baptism, though they might have worn it for the Eucharist. There were others who disapproved of the use of the surplice altogether. But for Herbert it is clearly a matter of importance for the *sacrament of baptism*, and no doubt he interpreted the priest's use of the surplice as a symbol of the white garment of resurrection, of having put on Christ (Gal. 3:27).

Secondly, baptism is to take place on Sundays or festivals. In this he was agreeing with those Puritans who resisted privatizing baptism, and in the previous chapter we saw how Andrewes made this point as well. Baptism must not normally be on demand. The Puritan reason would have been the desire to baptize whenever the congregation is gathered. Herbert's – and Andrewes' – was that the Sundays and festivals are for corporate observance and celebration. It is entirely in the spirit of the Prayer Book that baptism should regain its traditional position as part of the normal worship of the Christian community.

Thirdly, the names chosen are of some importance and therefore the parson should intervene when these might be trivial or meaningless. As we shall see in his two poems on baptism in *The Temple*, for Herbert the Christian name is of great significance.

Fourthly, of all the prayers in the baptism service on which he could comment, he singles out that which gives thanks for the providence of God in bringing us to the point of baptism. This prayer comes between the reading of the Gospel Passage (Mark 10:13–16) and the renunciations. Here is the version which appears in the 1662 Prayer Book:

Almighty and everlasting God, heavenly Father, we give thee humble thanks, that thou hast vouchsafed to call us to the knowledge of thy grace, and faith in thee: Increase this knowledge, and confirm this faith in us evermore. Give they holy Spirit to this Infant, that he may be born again, and be made an heir of everlasting salvation; through our Lord Jesus Christ, who liveth and reigneth with thee in the Holy Spirit, now and for ever. Amen.[14]

Interestingly, the version of this prayer with which Herbert was familiar only has 'call us to knowledge of thy grace' (not 'to the knowledge'). Although there were many editorial alterations to the Prayer Book at the Restoration, and many reasons can be given for them, it is tempting to suggest that the insertion of 'the' before 'knowledge' is the result of someone reading Herbert at this point. Herbert seems to single out this prayer for the specific reason that it speaks of God's providence, his fore-knowledge of us.

Fifthly, the priest 'willingly and cheerfully' makes the signing of the cross. We have already encountered this controversy and we shall see it again in Herbert's Latin poem in reply to Andrew Melville's attack on Prayer Book practices. We have suggested before that there were Puritan clergy who omitted this ceremony altogether. For Herbert it is something to do willingly and with enthusiasm, because so far from being sinister it is holy and meaningful.

Sixthly, the godparents are to be instructed on their duties for the child. And note the context: in God's presence, and in the communion of saints, and in that strength, undertaking a duty on behalf of a Christian soul. Godparents therefore do not exist in isolation. They should feel encouraged by the strength of God and the whole company of heaven.

Finally, 'He adviseth all to call to mind their Baptism often . . .' For Herbert, baptism is central and it marks the beginning of the Christian life. Because of that, people should call to mind their baptism, and one of the best ways of doing so is to be present at someone else's baptism, which is the teaching of the Prayer Book itself. Between these lines, we can read of a corporate view of baptism in which Herbert tries to inculcate in his readers a less individualistic approach to this fundamental sacrament of the Christian faith. He ends this section by suggesting that baptism should not be reduced to basic principles but lived out according to its duties and the vows made on our behalf by others. It is not for nothing that he repeats the three words, 'their baptism often'.

It is good to balance the quiet and firm simplicity of these recommendations against the rich and sometimes overtly controversial discussions of Perkins and Hooker, and the rich textures of Andrewes' preaching. One senses here that if a priest wants to put into practice the theology of Hooker and Andrewes, he does so in the kind of way that Herbert recommends.

Herbert's *The Temple* was published in 1633. It is not a historical theologian's task to enter the complex fray of literary criticism concerning these poems – except to note their complexity.[15] There have been many debates about the structure of *The Temple*, and even how far George Herbert was a crypto-medieval Catholic, and how far a strong Puritan. On the basis of what we have seen written in *The Priest to the Temple*, it is hard to locate Herbert's ultimate ecclesiastical place anywhere else than in the Prayer Book, Anglican, parish priesthood.

There are two poems about baptism which come after the Holy Week and Easter sequence in *The Temple*.[16] But before we look at them, it may be useful to note the wider baptismal context in which these poems seem to be placed. After the opening poem ('The Dedication'), there is the long poem entitled 'The Church-porch' which is a lengthy meditation on the beginning of the Christian life and its repeated renewal within a person's life. It is, therefore, not for nothing that a poem positioned, as it were, at the church porch, should have as its second stanza:

> Beware of lust: it doth pollute and foul
> Whom God in Baptisme washt with His own blood.
> It blots thy lesson written in thy soul;
> The holy lines cannot be understood.

How dare those eyes upon a Bible look,
Much lesse towards God, whose lust is all their book?

This verse is about repentance, and it is not a coincidence that Herbert should state that essential contrast between the gift of redemption by the blood of Christ given in baptism and the life of the sinner who can be redeemed.

Then, after the 'Church-porch' poem there is the 'Superliminare':

> Thou, whom the former precepts have
> Sprinkled and taught, how to behave
> Thy self in church; approach, and taste
> The churches mysticall repast.[17]

This poem seems to act as a bridge between the porch and entry to the church, which is the next section, beginning with a poem called 'The Altar'. In these four pithy opening lines, we do indeed seem to turn from the font to the altar. The font is where we were washed (sprinkled) and every time we enter the church building, physically or spiritually, we have a chance to renew that sacramental presence in us before we go to the altar for the Eucharist. The baptismal function of this verse, and indeed of the verse in the previous poem, cannot be overestimated. If Herbert is a eucharistic poet in *The Temple*, then he is also a thoroughly baptismal one. As if to underline this emphasis from the point of view of Herbert's vocation as a poet, the two poems entitled 'Jordan', which come much later, serve the function, in the words of Elizabeth Clarke, 'to baptise poetry into the service of Christ'. For both poems express a strong suspicion of poetry for poetry's sake and yearn for a purified poetry that will say no more than needs to be said, as the third stanza of the first 'Jordan' poem states:

Shepherds are honest people; let them sing:
Riddle who list, for me, and pull for Prime:
I envie no mans nightingale or spring;
Nor let them punish me with losse of rime,
Who plainly say, *My God, My King.*[18]

With this wider background, it is appropriate now to look at the two baptism poems. These come much earlier, and appear together straight after the poem entitled 'Easter-wings'. There are a number of paired poems in *The Temple* and it is significant that Herbert should place these two baptismal gems after Easter, as if making the point that Easter and baptism are specially connected. Such an insight is nothing new but it shows Herbert's standing in that long line of tradition going back to the Fathers.

Here is the first poem:

As he that sees a dark and shadie grove,
    Stayes not, but looks beyond it on the skie;
    So when I view my sinnes, mine eyes remove
More backward still, and to that water flie,

Which is above the heav'ns, whose spring and vent
    Is in my deare Redeemers pierced side.
    O blessed streams! either ye do prevent
And stop our sinnes from growing thick and wide,
Or else give tears to drown them, as they grow.

In you Redemption measures all my time,
    And spreads the plaister equall to the crime.
You taught the Book of Life my name, that so,
    What ever future sinnes should me miscall,
    Your first acquaintance might discredit all.[19]

What can we glean from this poem? The first verse contrasts the 'dark and shadie grove' with the sky and makes another contrast between the sense of sinfulness and the font itself. The use of the expression 'More backward still' may suggest the jerk of the head to look further up into the sky and also the mind going back to the font, the moment of baptism – a motif emphasized, as we have already seen, in *The Priest to the Temple*. The source of forgiveness is the pierced side of Christ, who was celebrated in the Holy Week sequence of poems as crucified and also risen. The 'blessed streams' of water and blood from the side of Christ go ahead of us and forgive sins that have not yet been committed – hence the word 'prevent' – as well as letting sins grow almost like weeds. In the third verse we ourselves cry over our sins. But redemption is eternal and 'measures all my time'.

To illustrate this Herbert plucks a vivid verse from Isaiah: 'For Isaiah had said, let them take a lump of figs, and lay it for a plaister upon the boil and he shall recover' (Isa. 38:21). 'Plaister equall to the crime' is the work of Christ on the cross. God's providence, his fore-knowledge of us, is expressed in those sublime words, 'You taught the Book of Life my name'. It will be remembered that Herbert disliked the use of trivial names at baptism, perhaps because he believed that our names are written in the book of life. And the poem ends on a yet more powerful note, of God's prevenient grace and our eternal friendship with him – expressed at baptism itself.

The second poem has a different style:

> Since, Lord, to thee
> A narrow way and little gate
> Is all the passage, on my infancie
> Thou didst lay hold, and antedate
> My faith in me.

O let me still
Write thee great God, and me a childe:
Let me be soft and supple to thy will,
Small to myself, to others milde,
Behither ill.

Although by stealth
My flesh get on, yet let her sister
My soul, bid nothing, but preserve her wealth:
The growth of flesh is but a blister;
Childhood is health.[20]

Whereas the previous poem began with the image of looking at a shady grove, this one starts with the image of the
straight and narrow gate, echoing the prayer before baptism,
and Christ's teaching in the Sermon on the Mount (Matt.
7:14). But the person entering through this gate does so in
infancy, because 'Thou didst lay hold, and antedate/My faith
in me'. God's foreknowledge of us is so great that he believes
in us before we do. Herbert's use of the word 'infant' could
well be an echo of a Patristic custom of referring to the newly
baptized, whatever their age, as *infantes*. What he says of
'childhood' at the end certainly supports such a view.

The second verse bring alive the contrast between 'great
God' and the human race as 'a child'. In a line reminiscent
of 'incline my heart unto thy testimonies' (Ps. 119:36), the
life of the child of God is defined as being small to oneself,
and mild to others, except in the face of what is wrong.

The third dwells on the contrast between physical decay
and spiritual growth. For baptism is not just a baptism of the
body but a baptism of the soul, as Andrewes taught. That
bald statement 'Childhood is health' with which the poem
concludes leaves the reader in no doubt that the childhood
in question is to be a child of God, not a child of the world.
That spiritual growth which lies behind this poem is another

indication of the memory of baptism kept alive and celebrated throughout one's life.

The Temple made a profound impression on many people. Herbert's short and rich style with all its subtlety and its love of monosyllabic words went on to inspire poets and hymn-writers in later generations. In 1697 many of the poems in *The Temple* were turned into common metre hymns for use in Non-conformist worship. But neither of the two poems on baptism figured in this collection.[21] To delete baptism from *The Temple* is to deprive Herbert of one of his spiritual foundation-stones.

We now turn to a different and more controversial side of Herbert. Among his Latin poems are two concerning baptism which along with others act as a riposte against a sarcastic attack on Prayer Book worship written in Latin verse by the Scottish Reformer, Andrew Melville, in 1607. Melville had been a leader of the Presbyterian movement in Scotland in the previous century and had fallen foul of King James when he resisted James's attempts to give the bishops in the Church of Scotland a more powerful position. He was summoned to London in 1606 to appear before the King after insisting that there should be a free Assembly of the Church in Scotland. That small part of the poem which attacks baptismal practice singles out the signing with the cross, set prayers, questions made as if to a baby, and the practice of confirmation by a bishop.[22] There is nothing, however, in Melville's poem that is against infant baptism, as Stewart suggests;[23] Melville simply wants Scottish Presbyterian practice, no more, no less. He would have no sign of the cross, no set prayers, and no questions to godparents, but rather acceptance of the children of believing parents, within the covenant of grace.

Herbert replied to this with two Latin poems. The first is entitled 'Holy Baptism', and here is a fresh English translation.

When the tender infant is brought to the sacred waters
Do you find the words unholy because the child does
    not understand them?
Do we not buy fields so? And to fields the Redeemer
Himself compared the heavenly regions of God ever-
    lasting.
That is to say, if circumstances or too cramping age hold
    back the buyer
A friend stands in to supply the mandates of the law.
Perhaps you will also stop the infant from being carried
    to the waters
And want him by his own efforts to approach the
    temple's threshold:
But if, Melville, the child may ask for the feet of others
Why should another's voice meet with your displeasure?
Rightly you would supply to harmless unweaned chil-
    dren everything
Which reason, if grown up, knows on its own account.
What is to stop someone responding to the cries of a
    child
When it cannot itself utter distinct prayers?
You are savage, tearing the promises of heaven from the
    little ones;
And may it be that no-one stand surety for you when
    you ask their help.[24]

What are we to make of this? The answer is a great deal.
The poem defends bringing an infant to church, and promis-
ing the Christian faith on behalf of that infant, as one buys
a property on behalf of someone else. There is nothing wrong
with a friend standing in. To hold an infant back would
deprive it of great riches for the future. So it is proper to
approach the temple and to answer on behalf of the infant.
The set prayers are those which the child will learn in the
future. And both they and the whole baptism service are

about the promises of heaven, God's foreknowledge of us once more.

Then there is a shorter poem entitled 'The sign of the cross':

> Why do you insinuate such calumnies against the cross
>   which harms no-one?
> Evil-intentioned demons are put to flight no more readily
>   by the cross of Christ than are your companions.
> Heavy was the Apostles' guilt to have avoided the cross
>   of Christ as he breathed forth his spirit.
> And more, each Christian is called by Tertullian a fish
>   on account of the bath of water in which we are as
>   little ones washed.
> Who indeed can swim with their arms without the far
>   framed cross?
> But let us not waste time: for the cross will be yours,
> Whether you approve it or are against it.[25]

Just as Hooker made a great deal of defending the sign of the cross, Herbert singles out this particular practice. The cross harms no-one, far from it. It can dispel demons, and perhaps Herbert's waspish poetry at this point is thinking of Melville himself. The apostles were ashamed of the cross but that does not mean that we should be ashamed of it too. And if, allowing early Church imagery, the new Christian is likened to a fish, the cross will enable him to swim in later life. At the end of the day, the cross is a gift given to all of us whether we like it or not.

With these poems we are in an atmosphere different from Herbert's other writings. Melville takes Herbert straight into the fray of the Puritan – Prayer Book divide with all its controversy, anger, and point-scoring. But one can see the positive side of the debate from Herbert's point of view. Baptism is not something that we do to certain people on certain conditions. It is fundamentally an act of faith, faith in the providence of God, within an ordered liturgy, whose 'distinct prayers' may not be immediately comprehensible to the assembly, or even to the infant, but are there not for the moment but for the future. Similarly, the sign of the cross is so fundamental to the Christian faith that baptism is incomplete without it. We may not immediately like it but that may be more a reflection on us than on the tradition that places it in the liturgy in the first place. Herbert wants Melville – and others like him – to be more patient about practices which may at first sight seem difficult to understand, because he is confident that in the end they will make sense. He is not far from Hooker in this kind of approach.

Herbert is a baptismal poet and writer in love with the providence of God. For him, the gap between our knowledge of God's grace and that grace itself is supremely and finely met in Christ himself. For him, the parson has a unique place in ministering the things of God and his inner life is an awesome responsibility. Early on in *A Priest to the Temple*, and long before he comes to the chapter on the sacraments, Herbert reflects on the parson *praying*. As if placing baptism in the wider context of life that he achieves so effectively in his *Temple* poems, he observes that:

> This he doth, first, as being truly touched and amazed with the majesty of God, before whom he then presents himself; yet not as himself alone, but as presenting with himself the whole congregation, whose sins he then bears, and brings with his own to the heavenly altar to be bathed, and washed in the sacred laver of Christ's blood.[26]

That bathing and washing finds its sacramental expression at the font. On that basis, and on that basis alone, we can bear to bring infants to the font, and have our own baptism renewed, our own perspectives of eternity refreshed, our own life of faith reinvigorated. Herbert's vision is not a simplistic one, nor is it easy-going. It is about God renewing our lives again and again, as we enter the 'narrow way and little gate' that sets us on our way to heaven.

7

What About the Unbaptized?

John Bramhall (1594–1663)

The telephone rang at half-past three one morning in February 1974. It was the maternity ward of Grantham Hospital. A baby had just been born and the nurse on duty was asking if the Curate would come and baptize him as he was dangerously ill. I wiped the sleep out of my eyes, rapidly washed and shaved, grabbed some robes, and drove the short distance – about a mile – to the hospital. When I got to the ward, I was whisked into a room where the nurse stood next to an incubator. There was a bowl of water and I think I remember a cross, but not much else. On these occasions, one is not in the mood for being liturgically creative. I looked up my Prayer Book and extracted from the office of private baptism those elements deemed necessary for what was in effect an emergency baptism. The congregation consisted of the nurse and myself as the mother was recovering and the father had not yet arrived. I said the prayers, blessed the water, dabbed my finger in the water, put it through the open door in the incubator and dabbed a small amount on the baby's head. The signing with the cross had a particular significance on that occasion which I shall never forget.

When the short service was over, I blew out the candles, reverently disposed of the water, and went back and chatted with the nurse, as the mother was slumbering despite considerable pain, and there was no chance of my getting back to sleep if I returned home.

The nurse and I did not enter any deep theological discussion about why the service had taken place. We simply talked about the mother, the baby, and what it was like to work in the hospital. I am not sure exactly how the request for the baptism came in the first place; did the mother request it, or did the nurse make the offer to the mother? I do know that the mother knew that I was coming. I did visit her briefly in the ward before I went home, for by that stage she was awake and ready for a fleeting conversation. She smiled appreciatively. I think that she wanted to use every means at her disposal to secure the life of her firstborn child. The young lad did indeed survive. I contacted the local incumbent, who was Rector of a country group of parishes out on the fens, and left it at that.

It was my first baptism. I was still a deacon and therefore technically only allowed to baptize in the absence of a priest. I celebrated a few more such baptisms before I was a priest, including two babies who died, and whose funerals I took in each case. With one of them it was late in the afternoon, and the congregation consisted of the parents, as the young boy was twelve days old and had been rushed back into hospital. I remember a year later a routine visit to the same maternity ward and seeing the same parents, this time in circumstances which for them were happier and more successful. I shall never forget the brief smile of sad recognition on their faces as I entered. I was part of an episode that they preferred to forget. For me it was particularly painful too, for to baptize a baby and then take the funeral when one is already the father of a small child is to be brought up against life at its most tender.

Such scenarios as these raise important questions about the Christian faith. Why *was* I asked to baptize those children then? Three kinds of answer can be given. The first is based on *fear*. Unless the baby is baptized, it will go to hell. This view goes back through the collective memory of the Western

Church to St Augustine, whose view of original sin was such as eventually to persuade the Church – and parents – to shorten the distance in time between birth and baptism.[1] This view is eloquently expressed in William Langland's *The Vision of Piers Plowman*:

> For a baptized man may, as maistres tell us,
> Thorough contricion come to the heighe hevene –
> . . .
> Ac [But] a barn withouten bapteme may nought so be
>   saved.[2]

And it is this view that we saw in the background of Hooker's argument for the *necessity* of baptism.[3]

Another motivation for the request stems from *duty*. Baptism in these circumstances is a rite of passage, through which we all have to go, part of the way groups and societies operate at the religious level. It is not fashionable in many Christian circles to speak like this nowadays but it has certainly been the case in the past.

Then there is the third view, which is based on *hope*. The mother, frankly, hopes that baptism will heal the child, or at any rate provide some stay of execution so that she can enjoy the child at home even if only for a short time.

Questions such as these stand at the crossroads between the theory and the practice of the gospel and the sacraments. Baptism needs to be preached in the context of repentance and living faith, but that repentance and living faith often intercept with 'test cases', such as I have described above. To say that a child must be baptized is a positive way of saying that God's love and grace are irresistible. Fear of going to hell is the negative aspect of refusing it. To say that baptism is a rite of passage which is part of the structure of our common life is a way of saying that God is to be found and rediscovered in the routines that we have inherited. But to reduce that to a sense of duty and no more is a distortion of the gospel. On the other hand, to express the hope that baptism heals is to affirm that all the sacraments and sacramental rites flow in and out of each other, and that they all – Eucharist included – begin at the font. The downside, of course, is when healing is interpreted in terms of magical outcome, as a form of trying to manipulate the future.

But this is where God is to be found, not in the ideal world, but in the ordinary world. There is no point in having a slick and watertight 'theology of baptism' unless it meets the questions and the yearnings, and the fears and duties and hopes, of the people for whom these sacraments are designed, namely everyone.

Interestingly enough, we come across a bit of a test case tucked away in the form of a discourse in the published works of John Bramhall,[4] who was one of the most versatile and energetic theologians on the seventeenth-century scene. Born at Pontefract in Yorkshire, he proceeded to what was then Sidney College, Cambridge, and on graduation returned to Yorkshire, where he served as Rector of Eterington and was made a Prebendary of York and then of Ripon, which cathedral he served as Sub-Dean. He gathered a reputation as a scholar (he married a clergy widow who was in possession of her first husband's considerable library), a strong and lively preacher, and a man who could confront the religious controversies of his time.

It was in this latter context that he came to the attention of the Archbishop of York in 1623, after two public disputations at North Allerton with Roman Catholic priests. Thomas Wentworth, Lord Deputy of Ireland, then took Bramhall with him to Ireland in 1633, where he was consecrated Bishop of Derry. A vigorous follower of the

Hooker–Andrewes tradition, he ensured, for example, that the Church of Ireland required that the altar should be fixed at the east end of the church and not be a moveable piece of furniture.[5] Bramhall made enemies for such boldness and attempts were made to bring charges of high treason against him in the unhappy confrontational atmosphere of the Civil War. He returned to England in 1642, from where he fled to the mainland of Europe in 1644. There he stayed until the Restoration in 1660, except for a brief spell in Ireland in 1648. He was on good terms with the Royal Family in exile and gave communion to Charles II in May 1650 before his (abortive) trip to Scotland to take the Solemn League and Covenant. He also confirmed members of the Royal Family. He was an obvious choice as Archbishop of Armagh in 1661, an office which he held for only two years before his death in 1663. He replenished the Irish bench of bishops and did much to restore the position of the Church there.[6]

What, then, of this short discourse by Bramhall? It was first published in 1676 among the many others of his collected works. It is slim by comparison. Most were written mainly in defence of Anglicanism during his time in exile. We know that this short discourse was indeed 'written while in exile'. It was sent to Sir Henry De Vic, who was Charles I's Ambassador to the Low Countries from 1644 to 1648. During those four years, Bramhall spent much of the time at De Vic's official residence in Brussels.[7] De Vic was a devout Anglican who relished Bramhall's presence in Brussels, a presence which included regular preaching, celebrating the Eucharist, and taking confirmations in his large chapel, which was a haven for Anglicans in exile.[8]

It appears that this short essay is a kind of extended comment on a conversation that De Vic and Bramhall had at table. The topic of conversation was apparently the baptism of De Vic's daughter, Anne Charlotte. Exactly what form the conversation took and who else was present is not clear. From the tone of the opening it is clear that Bramhall had an understandably high profile in the discussion and perhaps the temperature rose higher than he would have wanted. 'This morning, lying musing in my bed, it produced some trouble in me, to consider how passionately we are all wedded to our own parties, and how apt we are all to censure the opinion of others, before we understand them; while our want of charity is a greater error in ourselves, and more displeasing to Almighty God, than any of those supposed assertions which we condemn in others; especially when they come to be rightly understood.'[9]

Those sentiments express much of Bramhall's personal style, one which T. S. Eliot described as 'a mind not gifted to discover the truth but tenacious to defend it'.[10] From a post-prandial argument about baptism, occasioned possibly by the birth of De Vic's daughter, Bramhall grasps the opportunity to hold forth for the first and only time in his (considerable) writing career on the subject of baptism. Like so much of his other work, written as most of it was in exile defending the Anglican cause, he is anxious to demonstrate the difference between the Anglican position (as he sees it) and that of the Roman Catholic Church. For this reason, one is led to expect that De Vic's motive for the baptism of his daughter was the fear that otherwise she would go to hell. This is not stated anywhere but it appears to lie hidden between the lines of this unexpected essay on what we would nowadays call 'theology in context'.

Bramhall begins by making three vital points: 'first, there is a great difference to be made between the sole want of baptism upon invincible necessity, and the contempt or wilful neglect of baptism when it may be had.'[11] Bramhall was not splitting a hair in making this distinction. People who are not in a position to be baptized are in a different category from those who have the opportunity and either despise it altogether or do not grasp it. Moreover, Bramhall notes that the Roman Catholic theologian Robert Bellarmine (1542–1621), with whom Lancelot Andrewes did battle on various issues, would not condemn those unable to be baptized upon 'invincible necessity', as Bramhall put it.

'Secondly, we distinguish between the visible sign, and the invisible grace.'[12] Here we are back on old ground. But Bramhall refuses to slide into the position taken, for example, by Perkins,[13] where the inward and the outward are distinguished to such a degree that they are almost driven apart. Instead, Bramhall asserts that those who have the visible sign receive the invisible grace. He insists that those who are not in a position to receive the visible sign may still by the grace of God receive the invisible grace. 'But whether God has so tied and bound himself to his ordinances and sacraments, that he doth not or cannot confer the grace of the sacraments extraordinarily where it seemeth good in his eyes, without the outward element, that is the question between us.' This is the nearest that Bramhall comes to revealing where he and De Vic have differed; presumably De Vic wanted to tie God to the sacraments after the traditional medieval Catholic fashion.

'Thirdly, we teach, that the case is not alike with little infants born of Christian parents, who die unbaptized without their own fault, and men of age and discretion; such as Nicodemus was, to whom Christ said, "except ye be born again of water under the spirit, ye cannot enter into the Kingdom of Heaven."'[14] Bramhall suggests that unbaptized *infants* are more likely to receive grace from God than unbaptized *adults*. This is a neat theological distinction with which it may be hard to sympathize although the context in which Bramhall was operating included a Protestant climate at home among whose ranks were those who were insisting that only adults should be baptized in the first place.

Bramhall proceeds to give five grounds for the last

assertion. And all are taken from within the Christian tradition. First of all, the grace of the sacrament is indeed communicable without the sacrament, as witness those early Christians who went to their deaths as martyrs without the opportunity to be baptized. Secondly, the *desire* for baptism was accepted in early times for baptism itself. (This is partially explained by the restriction of baptism to certain occasions, which he mentions later.) Thirdly, the medieval Schoolmen taught that abortive infants did not go to hell. Fourthly, Jewish children could be saved without circumcision, so that the uncircumcised were not excluded from the covenant. Fifthly, it was the custom of the patristic Church to delay baptism, because it was restricted to certain seasons, for example Easter and Pentecost.[15]

On their own, none of these points is entirely persuasive. Cumulatively, however, they produce a picture in which baptism holds a central and responsible place in the life of the Church. This relates to Bramhall's emphasis on 'internal' and 'external' communion in the church.[16] *Internal* communion is living fellowship within the local church, whereas *external* communion is the use of the same creeds, sacraments, and liturgical forms – which may vary from one church to another. In other words, for Bramhall the interior life of the Christian is not enough. Christianity is not exclusively a matter of private judgement. It is about being part of a community with all its weaknesses. But it is also about a loving God whose mission is – thankfully – far greater than the size or pedigree or impressiveness of a particular church at a given time. Baptism is crucial but it cannot be indispensable because only God is indispensable. This leads Bramhall, finally, to refute Augustine's assertion that only those baptized can enter the Kingdom of God.[17]

Bramhall's loyalty to the Prayer Book inevitably led him to uphold the practice of confirmation, and he made a discourse on this subject whilst in Paris.[18] According to Bolton,

Bramhall distinguished between baptism and confirmation – always a necessary business! – by affirming that in baptism the Holy Spirit is given for regeneration, whereas in confirmation, the Spirit is given for corroboration of the faith of the believer.[19]

What, then, are we to make of this 'forthright and not always judicious' churchman? (Or 'Dr. Bramble' as he was nicknamed by some of his antagonists?)[20] Whether or not one wishes a dinner guest to follow up a conversation with a short theological treatise is beside the point. In any case, one only has to think of the lengthy and almost over-subsectioned works of William Perkins to realize that in theological writing we are dealing with the human race – warts and all. Nevertheless, the fact remains that in Bramhall we encounter someone who has a mastery of logical arrangement when faced with a particular human predicament. He found himself in conflict, for example, with the philosopher Thomas Hobbes, because he refused to accept the principle of determinism.[21] For Bramhall, reason liberates – in all aspects of life, faith included – and this gives us a clue to the kind of world-view which he espoused, all the more remarkable, given the difficult circumstances of much of his episcopate.

We must remember that he was active as Bishop of Derry only from 1633 until 1642, and as Archbishop of Armagh from 1661 to 1663. In other words, he was a virtual exile for eighteen years, and at one stage was so poor that he was forced to auction fishing boats at Flushing. No wonder Bramhall saw the grace of God at work in the exceptional circumstances of human nature. No wonder he was prepared to take to task even his generous host in Brussels for apparently adopting an exclusive position on the sacraments of the Church. There is nothing academic or compromised about Bramhall's Anglicanism. His baptismal theology, like his understanding of God, elevates love above fear, response above duty, and healing above yearning. I wish I had had him beside me at table to talk with after those emergency baptisms in Grantham Hospital in the spring of 1974.

8

Holy Living

Jeremy Taylor (1613–67)

In the spring of 1977 Michael Ramsey, the former Archbishop of Canterbury, returned to Lincoln Theological College for some teaching.[1] For him it was a trip down memory lane. He came back to Boston Parish Church to preach. He met people whom he remembered with astonishing accuracy. But one particular event lives on in the local folklore. He asked if he could visit Horbling Church, which lies out in the fens south of Sleaford. This is where Ramsey's maternal grandfather had been Vicar and where he had been baptized. Now, as a very old man, he was returning to his roots. Striding into the church with that shuffling gait so characteristic of him, he walked round the font, and then stood and spoke to it: 'Oh font, font, font; this is where my Christian life began.'

In that curious and dramatic statement, Ramsey was making an important point. Baptism is sacramentally where the Christian life begins. It is at baptism that our new life begins and it is therefore from baptism that all other ministrations of the Church irradiate. The water that is poured over us at the font leads us into other contexts in which hands are then placed on those heads, at confirmation, or marriage, or ordination, or absolution, or healing, or commendation to the mercies of God. The script which the Church supplies for these other occasions varies according to the context. But the waters of baptism remain in the background for us, always the same.

This is one of the reasons why fonts can have a special hold on people. It is one of the reasons why I have always fought shy of using movable bowls, so popular among the Puritans and popular today. Fellowship within the Catholic Church – with those who were baptized before us – is much greater than the sum total of the group of people who happen to gather on a particular occasion. For the font is where we are made holy at baptism.

Holiness, of course, is an intangible quality. One cannot set out to be holy. But it is the calling of every Christian, indeed of the entire human race. 'Holy things for holy persons' as the celebrant has stated at every celebration of the Greek liturgy since the fourth century.[2] Moreover, holiness cannot simply stop with God, and possibly a few remarkable people here and there. We have to put holiness into words to celebrate that holiness, and to provide some kind of guidance for the way that holiness can be a mark of our lives. Holiness starts sacramentally at the font in *Holy* Baptism. Holiness, therefore, is for everyone. As Donald Allchin has put it, 'holiness is about a festival of joy, a dinner party to which all the most unlikely people are invited'.[3] And of all the great writers of the seventeenth century who wrote about making those links, no name stands out more prominently than that of Jeremy Taylor.

Jeremy Taylor[4] was born in Cambridge in 1615 and baptized in Holy Trinity Church where his father was a churchwarden. After a distinguished career at Cambridge University, he was made Rector of Uppingham in Rutland in 1638. There he no doubt came into contact with the famous public school which had been founded in 1584. During the Civil War, Taylor sided with the King, who had him made a D.D. for a work on the office of Bishop entitled 'The sacred order of episcopacy'. He was taken prisoner by the Parliamentary forces in 1646 while serving as an army chaplain with the King.

Regarded with great suspicion by Parliament, Taylor spent the years up to the Restoration in virtual internal exile, first at the home of Richard Vaughan, the Earl of Carbery in South Wales. Then, after a short spell in the Tower of London, he went to Ireland in 1658, to work in Lisburn and Portmore, south-west of Belfast.

During his time at the Earl of Carbery's residence at Golden Grove, Camarthenshire, he seems to have had little to do except write books. And out they poured.[5] Perhaps the most popular was that published in 1650 and entitled *The Rule and Exercises of Holy Living*, which was dedicated to the Earl himself. In this remarkable little book, which has been reprinted on many occasions since, Taylor demonstrates a readiness to put into plain and flowing prose central aspects of living the Christian life: care of our time, purity of intention, practice of the presence of God, sobriety, temperance, chastity, humility, modesty, contentedness, obedience, justice, civil contracts, and restitution, which leads him on in the final section to the Christian religion itself: faith, hope, charity, reading or hearing the word of God, fasting, keeping festivals, prayer, alms, repentance, and preparation for receiving the sacrament.

That final chapter leads into a series of other prayers. *Prayer* is the operative word, for Jeremy Taylor seems to have had the knack of writing a prayer for any occasion at the drop of a hat. Near the end of *Holy Living* we find one directed to be said on our birthday or the day of our baptism. (One suspects Taylor would have preferred the latter occasion but perhaps he is being kind to those unable to find out when they were baptized.)

O Blessed and Eternal God, I give thee praise and glory for thy great mercy to me in causing me to be born of Christian parents, and didst not allot to me a portion with Misbelievers and Heathen that have not known thee.

Thou didst not suffer me to be strangled at the gate of the womb, but thy hand sustained and brought me to the light of the world, and the illumination of Baptism, with thy grace preventing my Election, and by an artificial necessity and holy prevention engaging me to the profession and practices of Christianity.

Lord, since that, I have broken the promises made in my behalf, and which I confirmed by my after-act; I went back from them by an evil life: and yet thou hast still continued to me life and time of repentance; and didst not cut me off in the beginning of my days, and the progress of my sins.

O Dearest God, pardon the errors and ignorances, the vices and vanities of my youth, and the faults of my more forward years, and let me never more stain the whiteness of my Baptismal robe: and now that by thy grace I still persist in the purposes of obedience, and do give up my name to Christ, and glory to be Disciple of thy institution, and a servant of Jesus, let me never fail of thy grace: let no root of bitterness spring up, and disorder my purposes, and defile my spirit.

O let my years be so many degrees of nearer approach to thee: and forsake me not, O God, in my old age, when I am grey-headed; and when my strength faileth me, be thou my strength and my guide unto death; that I may reckon my years, and apply my heart unto wisdom; and at last, after the spending a holy and a blessed life, I may be brought unto a glorious eternity, through Jesus Christ our Lord. Amen.[6]

This prayer is in many ways a summary of Taylor's digestion of baptism into the Christian life. There is a strong emphasis throughout on the providence of God – hence his thankfulness at being born of Christian parents and surviving childbirth, which no parent took for granted in those times.

In the third paragraph, Taylor recognizes the reality of sin in the baptized life, including his life after confirmation, which he describes as 'my after-act' perhaps tactfully so at a time (1650) when episcopal confirmation was not generally available. And he goes on to ask forgiveness for what has stained his 'baptismal robe'. Such forgiveness will enable him to persist in obedience and discipleship, in which connection no bitterness should spring up inside his soul. And he ends by asking for a fruitful old age and a happy death.

In the previous year, Taylor had published an even more remarkable book, which is usually referred to as *The Life of our Blessed Lord and Saviour Jesus Christ*, or else, *The Great Exemplar*, which are the first words of the original title given it by Taylor himself.[7] In many respects *The Great Exemplar* stands in relation to *Holy Living*, because the earlier book tells the tale and reflects upon the life of Christ, and applies it to the Christian, whereas *Holy Living* presupposes the life of Christ in the background, which the struggling believer seeks to apply in practical and devotional ways. Taylor never does anything by halves and brevity is not one of his virtues.

The Great Exemplar is carefully structured. Each section tells the story of an episode in the life of Christ in the Gospels, which is followed by considerations upon those events and is concluded with a prayer. Then, at certain specific points, there are extended discourses on specific aspects of Christian living at the end of these sections. For example, the nativity of Christ ends with a discourse on the nursing of children, and the presentation of Christ ends with a discourse on meditation.

In the first edition, before the final prayer right at the end of the work, Taylor uses the conclusion of Matthew's Gospel (Matt. 28:19–20) as a way of discussing briefly the sacrament of baptism. It is ordained by Christ, as a way of entering covenant with our Lord, in which he promises mercy and forgiveness. This is not the only mention of baptism in the work – far from it. There is a particularly rich discussion of Christ's own baptism earlier on (Matt. 3:13–17) which clearly owes a great deal to the sermon on the baptism of Christ by Lancelot Andrewes discussed in a previous chapter. Here Taylor indulges in many of the same themes, such as the Trinity, the opening of heaven, and even the mournful noise of the dove.[8] In 1652, however, Taylor wrote a discourse specifically on baptism, which was incorporated into the second edition of *The Great Exemplar* in the following year. Evidently, he thought it was necessary to apply baptism in a yet more focused manner to the way it was practised and thought about among many people at the time.

However, because Taylor had placed the baptism of Christ and his temptation in the wilderness together, and because there was already a discourse on temptation, he had to place this newly written discourse on baptism after his lengthy discussion of temptation. He clearly wanted his readers to see baptism not as an isolated event but as part of the on-going life of the Christian. Fundamentally, Taylor's view of baptism is the same vision that we saw in Andrewes' sermon, namely of Christ himself transforming the waters of baptism and drawing us into the divine life of holiness. This may explain why in 1657 Taylor made yet one more addition to this part of *The Great Exemplar*, in the form of an old Syriac prayer, which was supposed to have been used by Christ at his own baptism, according to an old Syrian tradition.[9]

Taylor's discourse covers both the meaning of baptism and the baptism of infants.[10]

He begins by referring to the life-giving character of water both in the old and new creation, an approach which we shall see also adopted by Simon Patrick.[11] All that precedes Christ's baptism, whether in the Old Testament or in other religions, is preparatory and comparative, as is summed up in the following assertion:

> The Holy Jesus having found his way ready prepared by the preaching of John, and by his baptism and the Jewish manner of adopting proselytes and disciples into the religion a way chalked out for him to initiate disciples into his religion, took what was so prepared, and changed it into a perpetual sacrament.[12]

Then he enunciates six benefits of baptism, which he applies later on after his discussion of the baptism of infants.[13] Baptism draws the disciples into the Kingdom of God. They are adopted into a covenant with God. Baptism is a new birth, 'a Spirit of grace', and he mentions in this connection the tradition in the early Church of 'spiritual fathers and susceptors' to the catechumens, those preparing for baptism. In baptism all sins are pardoned, and this means pardon of sins yet to be committed. 'He that hath once entered in at this gate of life is always in possibility of pardon . . . in proportion to this doctrine it is, that the Holy Scripture calls upon us to live a holy life in pursuance of this grace of baptism . . . Baptism is the door, and the ground of this confidence forever.' Finally, baptism confers sanctification on the baptized.

> By water we are sacramentally dead and buried, by the Spirit we are made alive . . . The descent of the Holy Spirit upon us in our baptism is a consigning or marking us for God, as the sheep of his pasture, as the soldiers of his army, as the servants of his household . . . The Holy Spirit comes unto us the author of holy thoughts and firm persuasions . . . The Holy Spirit descends upon us in baptism, to become the principle of a new life, to become a holy sea springing up into holiness . . . Baptism does also consign us to a holy resurrection.

We can see here allusions to the signing with the cross with the military imagery of its accompanying formula in the Prayer Book, as well as the blessing of the water itself. Taylor resolves the dilemma of sacrament and experience by recourse to the same device we noted in George Herbert, the providence of God: 'That part which is wholly the work of God does only antedate the work of man which is to succeed in its due time, and is after the manner of preventing grace.' And the means of grace given us by God is nothing less than a guardian angel, which we shall come across again, in Taylor's liturgy.

The second part of the discourse concerns the baptism of infants. Taylor adopts the same approach to his subject, by much subdivision.[14] 'Baptism is the key in Christ's hand, and therefore opens as he opens and shuts by his rule.' In other words baptism is the act of Christ in his Church. 'Baptism is the first ordinary current in which the Spirit moves and descends upon us; and where God's Spirit is, they are the sons of God . . .' And he returns to the disjunction between the gift of the sacrament and the experience of salvation: 'baptism and its effect may be separated, and do not always go in conjunction . . .' But however important dispositions towards baptism are, they do not prevent the efficacy of the sacrament. 'Repentance and faith are not necessary to the susception of baptism', for, 'that actual faith is necessary, not to the susception, but to the consequent effects of baptism . . .' We cannot earn grace: 'no disposition, or act of man, can deserve the first grace, or the grace of pardon'. And yet baptism is not a one-off event: 'it is an entrance to a conjugation and a state of blessings'. For 'the Holy Spirit, which descends upon the waters of baptism, does not instantly produce its effects in the soul of the baptized . . . the Church gives the sacrament, God gives the grace of the sacrament.' Therefore there is no point in delaying baptism. He insists that children were baptized in the New Testament and refuses to accept the exclusively adult baptist position. 'Infants receive many benefits by the susception of baptism, and therefore, in charity, in duty we are to bring them to baptism.'

Taylor completes the discourse by applying the six benefits of baptism mentioned earlier: entry into the Kingdom of Christ, the covenant of the Gospel, being born again, receiving the forgiveness of sins, pardon for sins in the future and sanctification.[15] On the question of original sin, Taylor challenged the theological fashion of the day, which was strongly imbued with the spirit of Augustine. For Taylor, God must be love, therefore he cannot be so cruel as to inflict suffering deliberately on the human race. Therefore he could not speak of the total depravity of man, which was much further than Augustine was prepared to go in any case. Choosing his words carefully, he says: 'so it is in baptism; it does not heal the wounds of actual sins, because they have not committed them; but it takes off the evil of original sin; whatever is imputed to us by Adam's prevarication, is washed off by the death of the second Adam, into which we are baptized.'

Sacraments are vital for Taylor, because they are about equipping ordinary men and women to live better lives. 'Baptism does not so forgive future sins, that we may do what we please, or so as we need not labour, and watch, and fear, perpetually, and make use of God's grace to actuate our endeavours . . . What was lost by Adam is restored by Christ; the same righteousness, only it is not born, but super-induced; not integral, but interrupted.' Those who over-stress the fallen nature of the human race place an impossible distance between God and humanity. Those who want to restrict baptism to believing adults of their own kind run the risk of projecting their own culture on to the life of God: 'They limit the Spirit too much, and understand it too little, who take accounts of his secret workings, and measure them by the material lines and methods of natural and animal effects.'

In the concluding pages of this part of the discourse,[16]

Taylor recapitulates – something he loves to do at length. He mentions the guardian angel again and defends the baptism of infants on the basis of congregations for many centuries having been people baptized in infancy. He appeals to ancient Fathers to support the practice. And he even defends the practice of communicating baptized infants.

> And although the after-ages of the Church, which refuse to communicate infants, have found some little things against the lawfulness, and those ages that used it found out some pretences for its necessity; yet both the one and the other had liberty to follow their own necessities, so in all things they followed Christ. Certainly there is infinitely more reason, why infants may be communicated, than why they may not be baptized.

Taylor was to become an enthusiast for confirmation when he was made a bishop. But what of Taylor's understanding of baptism as expressed in this discourse? He is repetitive and long-winded – of that there can be no doubt. But he draws together a number of strands that we have seen in previous writers. He has the passion for numbering and sub-numbering that we saw in Perkins. He has the systematic clarity of Hooker. He has the homiletic flair of Andrewes, as witness his own direct borrowing in his discussion of the baptism of Christ. There is, too, something of the poetic about him. But the underlying trajectory of the holiness of God and the holy life to which we are called stands out with some considerable power. We are called into the Kingdom of Christ, to be adopted into the new covenant, to be given new birth, to receive pardon of our sins, including pardon of sins yet to be committed in the future; and, most crucial of all, we are called to be sanctified in the Holy Spirit. Of all the writers so far, Taylor perhaps emphasizes the power and working of the Spirit more than any other. But his writings also betray a sharper atmosphere of polemic than we saw in Perkins and Hooker, in that, from 1645, the Prayer Book was superseded by *The Westminster Directory*. This was the result of the meeting of the Assembly of Divines at Westminster to settle the path of church order and worship in the nation. Taylor made his own contribution in reaction to these provisions, and it is to this particular episode we must turn now.

The Westminster Directory contains a short form of baptism.[17] It begins by defining the practice of baptism, which is not to be undertaken by any private person, nor in any private place, but in the face of the congregation, 'and not in the places where fonts in the time of Popery were fitly and superstitiously placed'. The child to be baptized is to be presented by the father, or in his absence, some 'Christian friend'.

There follows a general instruction to be given by the minister which stresses the original sin being taken away by the blood of Christ, of which the water of baptism signifies that cleansing, but does not effect it. Children are admitted to baptism because Christ embraced them and took them into his arms (an allusion to Mark 10:13–17 – in the Prayer Book rite). The children are Christians and 'federally holy before baptism', and so the grace and virtue of baptism is not tied to the moment when it is administered. The minister admonishes all who are present to look back to their own baptism and to repent of their sins and ask for the right use of their baptism. He then exhorts the parent to consider the mercy of God and to bring the child up in the knowledge of the grounds of the Christian religion.

There follows a prayer for 'sanctifying the water to the spiritual use' and the sample text suggests the prayer might mention joining 'the inward baptism of the spirit with the outward baptism of water' – a theology Perkins would have espoused. It may also refer to 'other promises of the covenant of grace'.

The child is then baptized in the three-fold name, either by pouring or sprinkling of water, 'without adding any other ceremony', i.e. without any sign of the cross. There follows a prayer acknowledging the fact that 'the Lord is true and faithful in keeping the covenant and mercy', and baptism is described as 'the singular token and badge of his love in Christ'. It concludes with petition for the child 'to attain the years of discretion, that the Lord would so teach him by his Word and Spirit and make his baptism effectual to him . . .'

Apart from the prayer for sanctifying the water, this rite embodies much of the Puritan agenda that we have seen heretofore. The service must be public in every sense, which means at a main service, and at a basin, therefore not an old font. There are no godparents; there are no renunciations or promises, nor professions of faith; there is no sign of the cross – indeed, the description of baptism as a 'singular token and badge' of God's love could almost be taken as an implied rebuff of the sign of the cross. The rite expresses awareness of the tension of the inward and the outward aspects of the sacrament.

In 1658, Taylor produced his *Collection of Offices*, which is the nearest that he wrote to a complete Prayer Book. It was intended as a kind of covert Book of Common Prayer when this latter was proscribed.

In it there are prayers for all kinds of occasions and also parallel services to most of the offices in the Prayer Book, including baptism.[18] The baptism rite begins by directing that the water must be in a silver container, if at all possible, and the minister should be vested properly; that would be in sharp contrast to the *Directory*. There is an opening exhortation which mentions, like the *Directory*, the covenant of grace – but in this case no fewer than three times, and on the last occasion it asks that 'he may all his life walk in this covenant of grace and holiness as a lively member of the holy church'. Two prayers precede the Bible readings. They read very much like the opening discourse in *The Great Exemplar*: the first mentions water in the new creation and the old, and prays for the gift of rebirth, and the second begins by mentioning Christ's baptism in the Jordan and the sanctification of the water.

Two readings follow, the first being the account of Christ's baptism in Matthew 3:13–17 – the version which forms the basis of his treatment in *The Great Exemplar* – and the second that of Jesus receiving the children in his arms (Mark 10:13–17), as in the Prayer Book. A long exhortation follows, which stresses the love and mercy of God, and the need for children to be baptized. A prayer is then offered giving thanks for deliverance from the gates of hell and the sting of death, which asks that the child may be received into 'thy covenant of grace and favour'.

The godparents are now addressed in terms that stress God's redeeming grace. They renounce and profess in the interrogatory form of the Prayer Book. A long prayer for the child precedes the baptism itself, which is immediately followed by the signing of the cross. It is accompanied by a different form from that of the Prayer Book, obviously written in order to defend the use of the sign of the cross. Thanks are offered for the baptism of Christ and for the fact that the child has been received 'into the covenant of faith and repentance'; and the service concludes with some characteristically Tayloresque prayers, including one for a guardian angel for the newly baptized. Particularly evocative is the following prayer:

O God be thou his Father forever, Christ his elder Brother and Lord; the Church his Mother; let the body of Christ be his food, the blood of Christ be his drink and the Spirit the earnest of his inheritance. Let faith be his learning, religion his employment, his whole life be spiritual, heaven the object of his hopes, and the end of his labours; let him be thy servant in the Kingdom of Grace and thy

Son in the Kingdom of Glory through Jesus Christ our Lord.

Taylor's rite uses language that is redolent of the Prayer Book but is nonetheless in his own style. He uses the theme of the covenant of grace repeatedly, as well as the gift of regeneration, the presence and power of the Holy Spirit, and the sheer instrumentality and effectiveness of the baptism itself. Godparents take a full part and the sign of the cross is given full prominence. And underneath the rite, there still shines forth that prayerful confidence in the gift of holiness and holy living to God's people.

Taylor's views altered somewhat when he became a bishop.[19] It may be that the new situation in Ireland at the Restoration made it necessary for him and his episcopal colleagues to take a stand over confirmation. His 'Discourse of Confirmation' appeared in 1663 and it is probably the boldest of its kind on this subject published so far. In his characteristically flowing style, he regards the whole Church as actually *needing* confirmation. 'Until we receive the Spirit of obsignation or confirmation, we are but babes in Christ.' Confirmation is of ancient origin. It is not a sacrament, but it is nonetheless important! He studies the eastern and western Fathers, insisting that bishops are the only ministers of confirmation. He would like anointing with chrism to be restored and notes that it was used in the 1549 Prayer Book baptism rite. He is keen on confirming at an early age. There is little here that would not seem in embryo in Hooker's own defence of confirmation.[20]

H. R. McAdoo has probably done more to bring Taylor into the forefront of seventeenth-century theological studies than anyone else. Writing of *The Great Exemplar*, he wisely observes: 'Jeremy Taylor did not just touch on many areas of theology. Rather did he dig deep in many fields of divinity with an industry all the more amazing when the troubled circumstances of much of his life are taken into consideration.'[21]

What endures, then, from Taylor's legacy is a passionate understanding of the love of God, the weakness of human nature, and the interaction of Christ with that fallen but redeemed humanity. From the wide sweeping meditation on Christ's life in *The Great Exemplar*, through the detailed application of that life in *Holy Living*, to his beautiful but quaint alternative baptism rite (clearly intended as a substitute for the outlawed Prayer Book), his strengths emerge in their true colours. Perhaps more than any other writer, he stresses the work of the Spirit not only in the life of Christ but in the sacramental worship and 'holy living' of the Christian. What is done in church is important, because it relates directly to the meaning of the baptized life. Christ blessed the waters, and they are blessed at baptism. The Spirit marks us as Christ's own, and we are signed with the sign of the cross in consequence. The effects of baptism are not limited by our own consciousness, whether at the moment of baptism or in growing in the holy life, and that is why the Christian community stands alongside us with godparents. That holy life, moreover, is one in which the critical human faculties have their own part to play. It is perhaps his grasp of the truth that 'the Church gives the sacrament, God gives the grace of the sacrament' that enables Taylor to locate baptism as a necessary holy rite at the font, to find a place for the historic rite of confirmation as a way for the believer to profess that faith and have it strengthened by the blessing of the Church, and – above all – to see the work of God in Christ applied graciously in 'holy living'. Central, however, to Taylor's whole scheme is the *narrative* character of Christ's baptism, which we encounter both in his discourse and his liturgy, for this is how Christ is celebrated as our contemporary in history, *now*. Indeed, there is a Matthean axis in his writings here, starting from the first edition of *The Great Exemplar*, with its discussion based on Christ's command to baptize (Matt. 28:20) and its earlier discussion of Christ's baptism (Matt. 3:13–17), and continuing in his subsequent (and unique) use of that text in his baptism rite.

Many of these aspirations find eloquent expression in the prayer with which his discourse on baptism ends.

O holy and eternal Jesus, who in thine own person wert pleased to sanctify the waters of baptism, and by thy institution and commandment didst make them effectual to excellent purposes of grace and remedy; be pleased to verify the holy effects of baptism to me and all thy servants, whose names are dedicated to thee in an early and timely presentation, and enable us with thy grace to verify all our promises by which we were bound then when Thou didst first make us thy own portion and relatives in the consummation of a holy covenant.

O be pleased to pardon all those undecencies and unhandsome interruptions of that state of favour, in which Thou didst plant us by thy grace, and admit us by the gates of baptism: and let that Spirit which moved upon those holy waters never be absent from us, but call upon us, and invite us by a perpetual argument and daily solicitations and inducements to holiness; that we may never return to the filthiness of sin, but by the answer of a good conscience may please Thee, and glorify thy name, and do honour to thy religion and institution in this world, and may receive the blessings and the rewards of it in the world to come, being presented to Thee pure and spotless in the day of thy power, when Thou shalt lead thy Church to a kingdom and endless glories.

9

Disciples of Christ

Richard Baxter (1615–91)

When I was a curate over twenty years ago, a Youth Fellowship used to meet in my house once a fortnight. We discussed, we drank coffee, we ate biscuits, we sang and we prayed. Looking back on it, being with those young folk on such a regular basis was probably among the most enjoyable aspects of work at the time. At the end of what often felt like an endless Sunday, taking and assisting at services in different parts of the town, it was something of a relief to have that regular exposure to the stimulus and the questioning of the recently confirmed.

Every so often we would go away for a day and on one occasion we decided to go to the Cistercian Abbey of Mount St Bernard at Coalville in Leicestershire. Although it was only built in the nineteenth century, its atmosphere breathes the centuries of austerity of the Cistercian movement: farming, a vegetarian diet, and a very early start to the day.

The theme that we chose for that day was discipleship. We felt as a group that we wanted to look at our own following of Christ, put our own Christianity under the microscope, and think and pray further about it. Somewhat to our surprise, the monk who looked after us – a very ecumenically-minded man – said at the beginning of his first talk that he had been a bit puzzled by the word 'discipleship'. Then he thought for a bit and realized that although it wasn't much used by Roman Catholics, it was a term that meant a great deal to Churches of the Reformation.

Then he quickly added that he wasn't suggesting that Roman Catholics weren't interested in following Christ. It was simply that they might have used different terminology.

Be that as it may, we spent a day listening to our host, observing one another, and ending with a time of prayer, Bible reading and praise. It was interesting to see the effect of a monastic community on these young Anglicans, because for each one of them it was the first time they had darkened the doors of an abbey. I think that that summer Saturday probably remained with us for a long time. It was not a great moment of disclosure. But it marked one step along a journey – a journey of trying to follow Christ.

The word 'disciple' – literally in the Greek, 'learner' – occurs frequently in the Gospels and also in the Acts of the Apostles. Interestingly, it does not appear in any of the Epistles. Jesus' followers are assumed from early on in each of the Gospels to be his disciples. He keeps addressing them in different ways, apart from the crowd, and they remain his disciples after the crucifixion. In other words, to be a disciple of Christ is to be someone who is never let down by him. We may forsake him and flee from him (Matt. 26:56) but he is still ready to appear before us, and indeed to make the boldest demands of all on us, namely to go forth and baptize, and to make disciples of all the nations (Matt. 28:19–20).

Baptism and discipleship are closely connected, as we have seen again and again thus far. We need sacraments, but they are not the whole story. To put it another way, we cannot do without sacraments, for if we did, we would internalize the Christian faith, and the Church would become a collection of individuals and no more. Baptism is the beginning of our discipleship, but it cannot be the end. We saw earlier how William Perkins drove a wedge between the inward and the outward baptism in order to give as full as possible scope for discipleship to take effect.[1] Rather more astutely, Jeremy Taylor drew a distinction between the Church, which administered the sacrament, and God who gives the *grace* of the sacrament.[2] Moreover, it is easy to see why confirmation survived the Reformation into the Prayer Book, as a sacramental rite of Christian nurture. But there are always those who had no time for confirmation, and indeed many places where confirmation wasn't celebrated. Indeed, where the teaching and worship was Puritan in style from the reign of Queen Elizabeth I onwards, priests would baptize and later catechize the young, who would probably then receive communion. The bishop was not seen to be an integral part of Christian initiation. It was a local matter, in which the local parson took a key role in applying discipleship in the parish.

To juxtapose baptism and discipleship is to place baptism side by side with the Church's teaching ministry to the young. Baptism and discipleship mean accepting that the outward baptism has taken place, but that the inward baptism is either being looked for, or being built up or encouraged. Although many names could be associated with discipleship and Christian nurture perhaps none is more appropriate than that of Richard Baxter.[3]

'Get to know Baxter, and stay with Baxter, he will always do you good.'[4] This is how the Evangelical scholar James Packer ends a lecture on Baxter's life and work. In many respects he defies easy categorization. He was born in Rowton, Shropshire, in 1625. He was brought up in the Puritan tradition of the Church of England, and although he is frequently referred to as a Puritan, it needs to be recognized that he was an Anglican until the Restoration, when he left the Church of England. On opposite sides from Jeremy Taylor in the Civil War, he prospered during that time, with an effective and diligent ministry at Kidderminster. Such was his repute that his chair remains in the parish church, but the communion table was moved to the Congregational church, and his pulpit was placed in the Unitarian church – quite an ecumenical feat. He was offered the Bishopric of Worcester at the Restoration as part of the attempt to win over as many Presbyterians as possible to the new regime. He was himself keen on a 'reduced' kind of episcopacy but he evidently saw little chance of this succeeding. He was a Parliamentary appointment at Kidderminster, and he effectively deposed the sitting incumbent. Baxter was therefore himself extruded by the Bishop of Worcester at the Restoration. So began a period of thirty years as a freelance preacher and prolific writer in London. Although self-taught theologically, he wrote vast amounts of devotional material, including the well-known hymns 'Ye holy angels bright', and 'He wants not friends that hath Thy love'. Among his poetical works are to be found a series of verses entitled *Hypocrisy*. Here are two verses that demonstrate Baxter's strong Puritanism:

> Tradition, ceremony, pomp and rule,
> A human image without divine life;
> By Pharisees used as a tool,
> Of self-deceit and malignant strife.
>
> Thus they impossible communion make,
> And they damn all that do it not observe;
> None can tell for whom sovereign we must take,
> For which the Laws are from which none must swerve.[5]

And if those two verses are conjoined with the following, we know that we are in for an approach to the liturgy of baptism that is stark, rhetorical and deeply confident about the grace of God.

> I'll make a covenant with mine eyes,
> My tongue shall know its Law,
> I'll all the baits of sin despise
> And keep my heart in awe.[6]

Baxter himself experienced some of the tensions of his age surrounding Christian initiation in his own life-time. For example, he describes his confirmation by Bishop Thomas Morton, of Lichfield: 'in a Churchyard and in a Path-way, as the Bishop past by, we kneeled down and laying his Hands on every Boy's Head, he said a few words.'[7] Strange as that seems to us, it had been common in the Middle Ages for bishops to confirm outside, and even from horseback. Morton was no doubt following the High Church fashion of the bishops of the reign of Charles I to get around the dioceses and take confirmations. Baxter refers to the service as being 'Bishop't' – which was an old nick-name for confirmation. He did not think much of the practice. For him confirmation was personal commitment. We can read between the lines of the verse quoted above when they speak of making the covenant *my own*, with sight and speech, making a conscious decision to renounce sin, and keep the heart in awe of God himself. Baxter himself was a godparent at twenty-three, but soon came to shun the custom; and although he had doubts about infant baptism, he came round to a view that this was right. He was not, therefore, one simply to conform to the Prayer Book requirements without giving serious thought as to their theological and pastoral implications.

What of Baxter's liturgical practice?[8] Baxter gives an account of his procedure at Kidderminster, as follows:

> After the opening of the nature and use of the Ordinance, I require the parents (both, where they can come) to profess their own faith, by owning the common creed when I recite it, and by expressing that they take the Lord for their God and Christ for their Redeemer, and the Holy Ghost for their Sanctifier. And then I demand whether they desire this child to be baptized into this faith, and entered into this covenant with God the Father, Son and Holy Ghost

(renouncing the world, the flesh and the devil). And after engaging them to a careful education of it, and prayer for God's acceptance of the child to be devoted to him, and blessing of the Ordinance, etc. I baptize it and conclude with thanksgiving and prayer.[9]

Since it is Baxter's own account, we can note the deliberate emphasis.

The rite is didactic. It is addressed directly to the parents, not the godparents. The 'common faith' is recited by Baxter himself, clearly a reference to a creed. The reference to 'renouncing the world, the flesh and the devil' echoes the Prayer Book formula at the signing of the cross, though Baxter steadfastly omits this particular custom. His baptism rite, therefore, consists in exhortation, engagement with the faith of the parents, and prayer for God's acceptance of the child, followed by the baptism itself and a thanksgiving.

As Spinks has observed,[10] this rite seems closely modelled on that of the *Westminster Directory*.[11] But a much fuller service, which perhaps gives us a clear indication of the texts and language used in Baxter's prayers, is to be found in what is often called the 'Savoy Liturgy'. This was an unsuccessful attempt by Baxter himself to produce an alternative to the Prayer Book at the Conference held at the Savoy in 1661 at Parliament's instigation soon after the Restoration.[12] The purpose of the Conference was to consider certain proposals for revising parts of the Prayer Book, and to win over those unhappy with it. Instead of baptism and confirmation, Baxter provides an order for 'the celebration of the sacrament of baptism' and 'of Catechizing and the Approbation of those that are to be admitted to the Lord's Supper'.[13] The opening directions give the minister the final decision as to whether he is satisfied with the faith of the parents and their knowledge of the essentials of Christianity. The parents should 'person-ally own their baptismal covenant'. And again slightly echoing the *Westminster Directory*, 'the font is to be placed to the greatest conveniency of the minister and people'.

The sample text of the opening exhortation begins by stressing that we inherit original sin from Adam, but that in Christ the world is offered a covenant of grace which is solemnly entered into by baptism. The faith of parents is sufficient to draw infants into this covenant, but 'then they must own their baptismal covenant and personally renew it, and give up themselves to God, unless they will not be owned by Christ'.

The service proceeds with an interrogation of the parents, some of which echoes Baxter's earlier account: 'Do you repent of your sins, and renounce the Flesh, the Devil, and the World, and consent to the Covenant of Grace, giving up yourself to God the Father, the Son, and the Holy Ghost, as your Creator, and Reconciled Father, your Redeemer, and your Sanctifier?' There is a strong emphasis in these questions on the grace of God and the need to live the life of a disciple of Christ. (This comes across much more forcefully than in the Prayer Book, with its use of the Creed.) The baptism consists of a prayer for the child, followed by the baptism itself in the threefold Name, followed by a declaration that the child is baptized, and a prayer of thanksgiving.

The prayer for the child before the baptism and the thanksgiving after it are saturated with biblical quotations. Both prayers refer to the covenant of grace, and pray fervently for the future life of the child. For example, the first prayer has: 'be reconciled to him, and take him for thy Child, renew him to the Image of thy Son, make him a fellow Citizen with the Saints, and one of thy household.' The renewal of the image of Christ in the child shows Baxter's view, not dissimilar to Taylor's, that the imputation to sin that we inherit from Adam through our parents does not make us guilty, but places us in the position of needing – and being able to be given – the grace to live a life worthy of our calling. Hence, the thanksgiving after the baptism prays: 'let him grow up in holiness, and when he comes to years of discretion, let thy spirit reveal unto him, the mysteries of the Gospel . . .'

The service ends with an exhortation to the parents and then to the people. Each is littered with biblical quotations, and repeated references to the covenant of grace. The parents are exhorted to bring the child up to know Christ for himself, and the congregation are exhorted to think for themselves on the full meaning of their own baptism.

As far as episcopal confirmation was concerned, Baxter's own personal experiences were hardly favourable. It meant little to him personally, for there was no examination of his Christian faith, and all the bishop appeared to do was to walk along a churchyard muttering a set form of prayer. In fact, Baxter lamented this attenuation – as he saw it – of confirmation, and it must be remembered that it was not until 1662 that the Prayer Book service had a form for the renewal of the baptismal vows by those who were about to be confirmed. The kind of confirmation service, therefore, which Baxter experienced was that which appeared in the first two Prayer Books, which consisted of a prayer over the candidates and the laying on of hands, and little else besides. Baxter, on the other hand, wanted a fuller rite, with an examination of the candidates, and with prayer for their continued growth in the Christian life. But this should be done by the local pastor, and not the bishop.[14] Baxter's liturgical programme, therefore, represents a moderate Puritan approach. What, then, of his other writings?

In 1682, Baxter published a lengthy work entitled *The Catechizing of Families*.[15] Like all his works it is noted for a certain copiousness. By that time Baxter was an ailing man, an official 'Non-conformist', with leisure on his hands to write from a perspective askance of the Established Church. *The Catechizing of Families* deals with many aspects of family life at a practical level, such as faith, prayer, Christian morality, and the place of the Reformed Churches within the rest of Christendom.

As the title implies, the book takes the form of questions and answers, rather like the catechesis in his 1661 'Savoy' baptism rite. Through William Ames (1576–1633), another prominent Puritan, Baxter was influenced by William Perkins. This influence is perhaps more obvious in the format and style of *The Catechizing of Families*, where we can draw parallels with William Perkins' *A Golden Chain*.[16]

Chapter 45 is devoted to baptism and begins with the question, 'What is baptism?', to which the reply is as follows: 'It is a sacred action, or sacrament, instituted by Christ, for the solemnizing of the covenant of Christianity between God and man, and the solemn investing us in the state of Christianity, obliging us to Christ, and for his delivering to us our relation and right to him as our Head, and to the gifts of his covenant.'

We know where we are. For in that pithy sentence, we are told that baptism is a sacrament, that it solemnizes the covenant between God and humanity, it 'invests' us into Christianity, and it places us in a mutual relationship with Christ.

But why the washing? 'A soul in flesh is apt to use sense, and needs some help of it.' This leads Baxter to condemn idolatry in liturgy; and, along the lines we have seen in Perkins, he states that the covenant is ratified by the persons acting within it, who are God in Trinity, and the party being baptized, or in the case of an infant, the parent or owner. And he goes on: 'baptism is the bringing of this conditional promise, upon man's consent to be an actual mutual covenant.' The requirement is that the person 'truly believe in this God the Father, Son and the Holy Ghost, and present and resolvably consenteth to be his in these relations'. The outward sign of baptism is water, whereby the candidate is washed from guilt, bathed with Christ, and bound by God to be Christian. Infants are not personally capable of receiving both the sign and the grace, but they enter into the covenant of God by their parents' will.

He then explains in covenant terms why Jews in the old dispensation were brought into covenant with Abraham. So in the same way infants of Christian parents are brought into the covenant of grace. Should not such baptisms be delayed? No. 'Christ knows what is best: and he hath told us of no other door of entrance into the visible church regularly, but by baptism.' Children of *unfaithful* parents are not baptized. Baxter then runs away with himself in asserting, 'doubtless, with unfaithful ministers, baptism at age also would be made but a ceremony, and slubbered over as confirmation is now, and as customary going to the church and sacrament is.' This is indeed the Baxter of 1682, lamenting the Restoration Church, with easy baptism, godparents, and episcopal confirmation. Before being admitted as a communicant, those baptized should be diligently catechized so that they can solemnly own and renew the baptismal vow and covenant, as if it were now to be first done. And he asserts, 'I think that the church is more corrupted for want of such a solemn, serious renewing of the baptismal covenant at age, and by turning confirmation into a ceremony, than by those anabaptists, who call people to be seriously re-baptized . . .' Baxter, however, is opposed to re-baptism. 'To be baptized again implied an untruth, that we were not baptized before.' (This is the same reason offered by Hooker.[17]) Baxter insists on 'the same covenant of grace which is made with infants and adults'. And he goes so far as to assert that 'if I thought infants had no visible right to remission in which baptism should invest them, I durst not baptize them. I think their holiness containeth a certain title to salvation.'

Then comes the telling question, 'How can infants be disciples that learn not?' Baxter replies that Christ sent his followers to make disciples of all nations, 'of which infants are a part'. 'Christ was our Teacher, Priest, and King in his infancy, by right, relation, and destination, and undertaking, and obligation to what he was asked to do; and so many infants be his subjects and disciples.' Discipleship is for all people, regardless of age. 'The child is in the covenant as the child of a believer devoted to God.' And he will have none of godparents. 'The further you go from a parent the darker is the case.'

Then comes the profession of Christian faith, which we noted Baxter used as Kidderminster, and also directs in the 1661 'Savoy' rite. The Church 'required the profession of a saving faith and repentance; and all the form of baptism used in England, and the whole Christian world, so happily agreeth in expressing this, that whoever will bring in the opinion, that the profession of a faith short of that which hath the promise of pardon and life, entitleth to baptism, must make a new baptismal form'. He rejects the view that infants should be baptized 'on a promise that they shall believe at age, and so have the benefits of baptism at age'. He insists that children are part of the covenant from baptism onwards.

Finally, Baxter lists the *uses* of baptism. These are a sense of our state of sin, a thankful sense of the grace of God, a faithful remembrance of that covenant which we sealed, knowledge of the baptismal covenant which tells us what Christianity is, a knowledge of what true conversion is, a knowledge of what the Catholic Church is, and a knowledge of how to exercise church discipline. Baptism 'is the very kernel of the Christian religion, and the symbol, or livery, of the church and members of Christ'. 'Baptism is to Christianity what public matrimony is to marriage, ordination to the ministry, and listing to a soldier, and crowning to a king.' There is no doubting the high view that Baxter has of baptism.

'Richard Baxter exemplified the plain, direct, yet emotionally charged, Puritan style, seeking for a verdict from his congregation.'[18] Such is the view of Horton Davies on Baxter's preaching style, but it could equally be held true of his approach to the great central sacrament of baptism and its working out in Christian nurture. His prose, though as lengthy as Perkins', has the same simplicity of style. There is no apparent desire for artistry, such as we saw in Hooker or Andrewes or Taylor. Like Perkins, he stands within the Puritan tradition, which will have nothing to do with godparents or the signing of the cross, and which concentrates on a theology of baptism based on the covenant of grace. We saw this motif as central to Perkins. It is mentioned by Hooker and Andrewes, though not held by them to be so central. Taylor managed to incorporate such a 'federal theology' into a more elaborate liturgy, and within a baptismal policy less restrictive than Baxter's. Although comparisons can be drawn between Baxter and Taylor,[19] it is their views of the Church and of the character of Christian liturgy that are so different. Taylor's liturgy begins with open arms, and his discussion of baptism has an almost iconographic devotion to the event of Christ's baptism. Baxter, on the other hand, starts his baptismal rite by drawing attention to those cases where the minister must not feel compelled to baptize; and while he is strong on the grace given in baptism, there is still an episode yet to come, when the growing Christian will own the baptismal covenant for himself. Similarly, while both Taylor and Baxter insist on confirmation, for Baxter it is primarily an act or commitment, whereas Taylor sees it as a means of the Church conferring grace through the ministry of the bishop.

Whereas Taylor's emphasis on Christ's baptism brought its own insistence on rebirth in the Holy Spirit, Baxter's central motifs are the washing away of sin and owning Christ for ourselves.

Taylor and Baxter inevitably stand in some relationship with other.[20] Culturally, the Anglican in Taylor and the Puritan in Baxter represent the tensions that eventually fragmented the Church of England in 1662. But there is more to the Puritan tradition than what happened at the Restoration. Baxter as a spiritual grandson of Perkins inherited a great deal of the Puritan protest at liturgical formality, and its insistence on ordinary Christian discipleship. Baxter could not simply balance liturgy with holy living like Jeremy Taylor, for with his more restrictive view of the Church came a wonderful confidence in the grace and mercy of God. Moreover, Baxter's perspective on discipleship, so apparent in everything that he wrote about baptism, and manifested by the outpouring of his literary works, is testimony to the never-ending nature of life in God, in which there is always more to learn, more to be thankful for, and more to believe in.

10

Professing the Faith

Simon Patrick (1626–1707)

I have sat through many confirmation sermons in my time, and now I find myself having to preach them myself. Whatever is said from the pulpit at the service itself or given in the form of instruction in confirmation groups only makes sense if it is the result of a conversation. After all, the only reason why a bishop has a throne is that the bishop was in the early centuries regarded as the *preacher* who sat in his chair and instructed his flock. That is why there are some bishop's chairs – for example, that in Metz Cathedral – which go right back to those early times, when the east end of the church was semi-circular ('apsidal'), with the bishop as preacher sitting in the centre. That chair owes its origin to the 'chair of Moses' in the synagogue. From here the address was given, as happened when Jesus went to Nazareth and sat down to preach after the passage of scripture had been read out (Luke 4:16–21). Jesus shows in the Gospels that preaching, however eloquent, has to result from some kind of contact with the community concerned. Sermons preached in a vacuum are seldom effective, even if they are published afterwards. The living word has to reach people's hearts and result in conviction, not just knowledge.

There are occasions when I am able to meet the candidates for confirmation beforehand and talk with them. This is particularly easy at the Saturday evening baptism and confirmation liturgies that take place in Portsmouth Cathedral at various times in the year. After the rehearsal, I am able to be with them on my own. Although I may know some details of which parishes the candidates come from, and what their ages are, I am never quite sure what I am letting myself in for. There are nearly always candidates who have to be baptized as well, which makes the service richer still, because we can gather around the font, which is placed in the centre of the building on the floor. Generous amounts of water can be used! Sometimes I have asked the candidates during the rehearsal to say something about themselves, to express in a few words what the occasion means to them. What they say can be very moving. With a group of about twenty candidates, there will be a mixture of ages, interests and temperaments. A young adult convert from one of the suburbs will be full of commitment to Christ. A nine-year-old girl from the inner city will say that she loves Jesus but feels a bit nervous. A much older person from a village will look back on a long and winding pilgrimage that somehow brought her to the present moment.

These snatches of human words are *professions* of the Christian faith.

To 'profess' means to declare and own. Baptism liturgies have always been at their most effective when they have managed to express what that Christian profession is, and lead the whole congregation – not just those directly involved in the baptism – to further exploration and renewed discipleship. The New Testament does not give us a uniform picture and there is not always an explicit declaration of the Christian faith on the part of the person being baptized. For example, when Philip meets the Ethiopian eunuch (Acts 8:36–8), Philip's baptism candidate doesn't explicitly state his belief in the Christian faith. But when Lydia is baptized after hearing Paul's preaching, she says, 'If you have judged me to be faithful to the Lord, come to my house and stay' (Acts 16:14–16).

In time the Church developed a creed, based on the interrogatory form, 'Do you believe in God the Father ... the Son ...
the Holy Spirit?' If one takes a very broad view, there has
always been what might be called a creative tension that
permeates the wider picture of what the Church teaches and
how human beings digest and experience it.[1]

We have seen so far the different ways in which this tension
was dealt with in the early days of the Prayer Book tradition.
For William Perkins, proper instruction in the Christian faith
came first,[2] whereas Richard Hooker adhered to the interrogatory form of the Apostles' Creed in the baptismal liturgy.[3]
Richard Baxter, on the other hand, had his own version of the
creed, which he used at baptism and confirmation,[4] whereas
Jeremy Taylor followed the Prayer Book, like Richard
Hooker.[5] Much more recently, the Church of England has
been looking into the possibility of allowing personal testimonies to be made at confirmation, and at the baptism and
confirmation of adult candidates.[6]

The *profession* of faith is, therefore, fundamental to the
baptism service. Its importance cannot be exaggerated, provided that all our rhetoric about a faith that is articulate and
coherent starts not with our own brains and tongues but with
the gift of God in the first place. Every single one of the writers
that we have looked at so far, including George Herbert the
poet,[7] places due and proper emphasis on the profession of
Christian faith. But not one of them uses the term so frequently as that rather neglected figure, Simon Patrick.[8]

Simon Patrick has been described as the 'doyen of the
devotional writers on the sacrament'.[9]

Certainly his works on the Eucharist are impressive for
their range and scope, starting with the *Mensa Mystica* in
1660, going on from *The Christian Sacrifice* (1670), through
A Book for Beginners and Help to Young Communicants
(1679), and finally the course of sermons preached in 1683

at Peterborough Cathedral where he was Dean, which was published as *A Treatise of the Necessity and Frequency of Receiving the Holy Communion* (1684).[10] But the fact is often overlooked that his first published work was the *Aqua Genitalis* [Water of Rebirth], *a Discourse concerning Baptism* (1658).[11] An author's first published work is of some personal significance.

Patrick was born in Gainsborough, not far from Lincoln, in 1626. He went up to Queens' College, Cambridge in 1644 where he came under the influence of a group of theologians often referred to as the Cambridge Platonists.[12] People like Patrick's mentors, John Smith and Ralph Cudworth, were critical of Puritan tendencies. They saw the present world as a fallen copy of the heavenly. They stressed the importance of reason in religious enquiry. However, their view of reason was not a cerebral one but was coloured by an emphasis on what we would nowadays call 'the religious imagination'. Patrick used such an approach to the fullest in his devotional writings. For example, in his *Advice to a Friend*, he writes, 'is Christ's death to excuse us from Holy Living?'[13] And in his *Discourse Concerning Prayer* he writes, 'nothing alters us so much as serious prayer, which puts a new mind into us, and for the present makes us quite another sort of creature.'[14]

Patrick's prose has the fluency of Taylor's without its efflorescence. When people consider seventeenth-century religious literature, they will often think of John Bunyan's *Pilgrim's Progress* (1678), but Patrick beat Bunyan to it fourteen years earlier with his *Parable of the Pilgrim* (1664).[15] Not as original as Bunyan, Patrick pioneered the genre, the narrative of the pilgrim on his way to Jerusalem, faced with temptations on every side, and making resolutions to pursue his journey of faith by the grace of God. A particular feature of Patrick's narrative are the spoken words, in which Pilgrim at length professes his Christian faith, a faith tested by and rooted in his experiences.

What of Patrick's career subsequent to Cambridge? He was made a Fellow of Queens', but like a number of those ordained – as they had to be then – as Presbyterians, he had doubts about the validity of what had taken place, particularly after reading Herbert Thorndike, whom we shall look at later. On 5 April 1654 he was ordained privately according to the Anglican rite by Joseph Hall, the deprived Bishop of Norwich, himself a theological and devotional writer of some stature. In the following year he left Cambridge and became domestic chaplain to Sir Walter St John at Battersea Manor, for his position at Cambridge had clearly become difficult. In 1657, he vacated his Fellowship and became Vicar of St Mary's in Battersea, and it was in those twilight years of the Commonwealth that the *Aqua Genitalis* was produced. The Restoration saw Patrick preferred to a Canonry at Westminster Abbey, and made Dean of Peterborough. After the accession of William III and Mary II, he was made Bishop of Chichester in 1689, and two years later, Bishop of Ely. Portraits of him reveal a man who was warm but tough, and this holds true of his writings.

Aqua Genitalis was published on 6 November 1658. It takes the form of an address to the reader, a preface, the main body of the text, and a short appendix on the evidence for confirmation. In his autobiography, Patrick tells us that the work started life as a sermon delivered at All Hallows' Church, Lombard Street, on 4 October of that year, only a matter of weeks before. The occasion was the baptism of the son of a minister in Lombard Street, the Revd. E. Vaughan. In the address to the reader which prefixes the work, Vaughan tells of the good reception given to the sermon on the occasion of his son's baptism and the importance of 'the begetting of right apprehensions of baptism in these days of so much contest'. When Vaughan himself requested that it should be printed, Patrick extended it in such a way that the concluding section might 'persuade to a Confirmation of the Baptismal Vow'.

The Prayer Book order of baptism would have been proscribed at the time. We therefore need to read *Aqua Genitalis* in the search for possible hints of where Patrick stood over controversial areas, such as baptism policy, godparents, the sign of the cross, the renunciation and the profession of faith, the blessing of the water, and what kind of font should be used. Patrick does not disappoint in this regard.

The preface begins with a typical Platonism: 'all this world below is but the image of the world above'. It continues by asserting the importance of sacraments from their psychological impact: 'rhythms which make a pretty noise or jingle are sooner affixed in people's minds than words and prose.'[16] Baptism is the 'sacrament of re-generation, or the second birth' – no surprise, in view of the title of his work! He makes much of the powerful symbolism of water. In referring to the controversy about infant baptism, he maintains that if people thought of the ends of baptism, then there would be fewer disputes. This suggests the construction of the discourse itself.

The main body of the discourse[17] is divided into a discussion of the meaning of baptism and its uses, an approach similar to those of Perkins and Taylor, though his theology resembles Taylor more than Perkins. It is hard to detect any 'ribs' which might suggest where the original sermon is to be found in this narrative, though I would hazard a guess that it began with the uses in the latter part, since at that stage Patrick begins to repeat himself. He was always a very practically orientated preacher. Significantly, Patrick chooses as his text the words '. . . and was baptized, he and all his, straight way' (Acts 16:33), from the baptism of the jailer by Paul and Silas. That suggests the *immediacy* of baptism and indicates a view of baptism that is anything but restrictive. He sets those words within the context of Christ's command to 'Go and teach all nations, baptizing them in the name of the

Father, Son, and Holy Ghost' (Matt. 28:19), and he contends that the words which follow, 'I am with you always to the end of the world' (Matt. 28:20), are baptismal. Christ is with his disciples in 'the work of the new birth'. This is a significant exegesis, and, in the circumstances, a fitting and convincing one.

Patrick's basic definition of baptism is summed up thus: 'I believe we shall find that to be baptized expresses something on our part, and something on God's; both which put together maketh it a federal rite, wherewith we and God enter into a covenant and agreement together, and mutually engage to the performance of several things which are all to our behoof and benefit.' This is the kind of federal theology we met in Taylor and Baxter. Baptism is therefore a 'profession of a religion whereinto we enter', and the words 'profession' and 'profess' occur again and again. Jews knew of 'divers washings' (Heb. 9:10). But this is a 'profession of repentance from dead works, from the devil, the world and the flesh' – and this leads him into describing the form of renunciation in the baptismal liturgy used in the old medieval rite. (He is aware of the tradition.) Baptism is also 'a profession of faith in the Father, Son and Holy Ghost', another indication of Patrick's reliance on the Prayer Book, however muted this would need to be in 1658. He defines this 'open profession' not just in terms of belief but as 'a profession of holiness and obedience'. In this connection he mentions the practice in the Byzantine rite of clothing the child immediately after baptism with a special formula. Profession of the faith in symbol is powerful for Patrick, as in the action of dying and rising, going down into the water and rising from it.

But for Patrick, baptism is also 'a profession of self-denial and taking up the cross'. He therefore defends the ancient practice of signing with the cross at baptism – a clear indication of his own conviction about the use of the sign of the cross. 'Our very first incorporation into Christ is in effect an expiration to the world, and when we begin to die then we begin to live.'

Baptism should be performed by an authorized minister (i.e. not anyone), and at the font, which, 'you know, used to be placed at the door or entrance to the church, to signify that by this we come into the congregation of Christ's disciples'. Patrick yearns for the traditional font! He mentions the practice of the priest holding the child in his arms and kissing it after baptism as the greeting of the holy kiss. Here again we see Patrick's appreciation of the wider liturgical tradition which had become either forgotten or forbidden in his own time. 'God receiveth us hereby into his family, to be numbered among his people, of whom he will have a special care.' This covenant is not burdensome, to the extent of being impossible, for God is always ready to receive us. He approaches a real moment of truth when he says that God 'admits us into that covenant of grace, which accepts of repentance instead of innocence, and of amendment instead of unerring obedience.'

Patrick's understanding of God's grace is evenly balanced. On the one hand, baptism is the 'promise of the Spirit, the infusion is likened to the pouring out of water, and so is in baptism most aptly signified and represented'. On the other hand, he insists that in baptism 'we receive hereby a promise of resurrection unto life'. Baptism *does* something, it is not just an outward ceremony. 'That conditional covenant of grace and mercy that was sealed before indefinitely by Christ's blood, is now sealed by baptism unto this particular person which receives it . . . In this second birth God is seized again of us, he owns us in a special manner for his children.' He seems sympathetic to the use of oil at baptism, 'to represent, I suppose, that God took him to be his son and bestow upon him the Holy Spirit'.

Patrick then asks, who are the persons to be baptized? Following the line going right back to Hooker (and beyond),

he insists that 'infants are capable to be engaged and pro-
fessed, and likewise to be received into the grace and favour
of God'. Infants are bound to have been baptized in the time
of the New Testament. He rejects 'the deniers of infant baptism' who want children dedicated to God but not actually
baptized, something Patrick finds incomprehensible, 'baptism
being the way wherein we devote ourselves to God'. He
refuses to lay too much of a burden on those baptized and
those presenting them: 'by this it will appear, that though a
profession of faith be required, yet not a distinct belief of
everything in Christ's religion, for that could not in the space
of an hour be comprehended.' For 'there are two teachings,
the one before, the other one after baptism'. Here Patrick is
on firm ground, for he has read the Fathers. His critical
respect for tradition enables him to move comfortably and
assuredly through the mass of evidence before him, as well
as the controversies of his own time. He does not expect
everyone to understand everything before the baptism actually takes place. Above all, he *trusts* the catechetical ministry
of the Church, and the reflective use of reason to interpret –
by faith – human experience.

Patrick now changes gear and turns, in the second part of
the discourse, to what he calls the four uses of baptism.[18] In
many respects this is a recapitulation of much of the material
we have seen so far. First, 'take notice of the great wisdom
of our Lord, that though he hath left us an outward ceremony
still in his church, it is such an one that signifies not one thing
but the whole religion; and not only signifies, but engages us
unto our duty.' The sacrament 'works' when it is celebrated
and continues to do so in the life of the believer. Patrick sets
great store by baptism as the rebirth from above, the dying
and rising of Christ, the gift of the Holy Spirit, the renunciation of evil and above all, the *profession* of that faith.

Then, 'take heed to yourselves and your ways according
to his word'. Those who are baptized must not run away

with the impression 'that the covenant of grace signifies all on God's part, and nothing at all on theirs'. For 'baptism, there only on the face, signifies the washing of the whole man from spiritual pollutions'.

Furthermore, 'we are in a covenant of grace; there is redemption for us if we have a mind to be delivered'. Patrick uses the image of the baptized as 'the soldiers of Christ', an echo of the Prayer Book formula at the signing of the cross, as a way of affirming Christ's presence with us, accompanying us on that journey in the power of the Holy Spirit.

But baptism leads inevitably towards confirmation. 'For the outward baptism, which is the visible sign and seal of the covenant, is not to be renewed; yet the answer of a good conscience (I Pet. 3:21), wherein the inward baptism doth consist, may, and ought to be reiterated, by a personal resumption and ratification of that vow which was made for us in our infant year.' Here we have the outward baptism and the inward baptism drawing closely together in the maturing Christian, but he does not write in such a way as to suggest – like Perkins – an innate conflict.[19] He cites the works of two divines who were famous at the time, but who left the Church of England at the Restoration for Non-conformity, Jonathan Hanmer (1606–87) and Richard Baxter. Both of them wanted to keep confirmation and use it as a way of *professing* the Christian faith.

Patrick sees confirmation not just as 'confirmation on our part' but as 'a receiving of God's blessing and grace by the hands and holy prayers of him that ministers, to strengthen us to perform our engagement, and make good our word and faith which we have plighted unto God'. In words reminiscent of Jeremy Taylor a few years later in his *Discourse of Confirmation*, Patrick contends that 'as in baptism the Holy Ghost was conveyed as a sanctifier, so herein as a comforter and strengthener'. Again and again that word 'profess' recurs. 'Our work is half done when we are heartily resolved; and more than half done when we profess these resolutions.' On a number of occasions in this part of the discourse, Patrick hints that the vows made in baptism are by godparents themselves. 'Cannot he that comes in the name of the child and sayeth "I believe" etc., "I renounce" etc., come and do the same in his own name? I really do think that they that are unwilling to undertake Christ's profession by an open promise would not be baptized if it had not been done in their infant years.' So enthusiastic is Patrick that people should be confirmed in order to receive Holy Communion that he calls in evidence from the first Prayer Books that the newly married should receive communion straight away.[20]

With some nostalgia he writes:

> ... let me speak to the very senses of vulgar people. Do you not remember the font stood at the lower end of the church, and the communion table up higher? Could you come from the one to the other but by the pulpit which stands in the middle between both? This teaches you (if you will learn) that you are only entered into the church, and are but in the beginning of religion by baptism, and that you must advance higher by being instructed and being taught in the faith of Christ, and can no otherwise be admitted from the lower to the highest forms of Christians.

Here can be no clearer indication of Patrick's yearning for the kind of architectural arrangement which was so dear to the hearts of men like Hooker and Andrewes, Herbert and Bramhall, earlier in the century.

But the final use of baptism is for 'all the people of God to live in love and peace together'. Here he touches on sensitive ground. 'We are not baptized into this or that particular opinion, nor received into a particular church, but into the belief of the gospel and into the church of God in general.' Baptism is about the unity of the Catholic Church, a unity which in England in 1658 was fragile indeed. He concludes: 'therefore let us live with them all as our confederates, as those that are tied together in the same bonds and united in the same covenant.'

So much for Patrick the parish priest in 1658. What of Patrick the Bishop of Chichester in 1690? In his Primary Visitation he asks, 'Is there a font of stone in your church or chapel with a cover to it, standing in the ancient and usual place? Doth your minister baptize there publicly? Is there a decent communion table in your chancel . . . ?' And he insists that the clergy should instruct the youth in the catechism, and prepare them for confirmation.[21] We can therefore see a consistency between what he preached and wrote in 1658 and what he asked of his clergy and laity in 1690.

When, therefore, we look in broader terms at the *Aqua Genitalis* we can identify a number of important features.

First of all, Patrick's liturgical traditionalism stands out. He likes the font near the back of the church. He wants godparents. He would like to use a baptismal rite that has the renunciation of evil as well as the profession of faith. He sees the sign of the cross as an integral part of the service. Because of his attachment to all the symbolisms of water, it is more than likely that he believed in its blessing as well. He is widely read, and knows of the practice of clothing the newly baptized in white and the use of oil, which give some credence to his concluding observation that we are not baptized into parts of the Church or particular opinions within it, but into the whole of the gospel of God.

There are other important features to note. That word 'profession' – to which he is so devoted – forms an important catechetical link between the sacrament of baptism and Christian nurture right up to confirmation and beyond. He does not believe in the supremacy of human effort but rather in the centrality of a holy life by the grace of God in response to his gracious and unmerited gifts. Baptism sanctifies, confirmation strengthens. Between that sacrament and the later sacramental rite there lie many different kinds of human experience, in which we are always able to discern the hand of God. That is why he knows full well that we simply cannot comprehend God at one single stage or moment.

Then there is the federal character of baptism. God binds himself to us, as we bind ourselves to him. Our binding ourselves to him is itself the action of God, reaching out to us in our weakness. The central assertion of the *Aqua Genitalis* is that God 'admits us into that covenant of grace, which accepts of repentance instead of innocence, and of amendment instead of un-erring obedience'.[22] At the heart of Patrick's baptismal theology is his understanding and love of the generous and gracious God. That gracious and generous nature requires a sacrament of baptism, and a further rite of confirmation, in which the *profession* of Christian faith is itself given, by the priest at the font, and by the bishop in the laying on of hands. (Tactfully Simon mentions nothing about bishops in the *Aqua Genitalis* since he was writing in 1658 when they had no jurisdiction whatever, but we may be sure of what was in the back of his mind.)

Patrick comes across as a traditional Anglican. The *Aqua Genitalis* is not a great and original discourse in the same league as Hooker's wonderful systematics, Perkins' endless outpourings, Andrewes' brilliant and imaginative exegesis, Herbert's succinct poetry, Bramhall's studied problématique, Taylor's streams of pastoral historical writings, or Baxter's deep pastoral directives. Here we have a theological parish priest's sermon writ large, trying to address the issues of the day, and in so doing capturing a vision of the Christian 'profession' – which is not just about words, but about redeemed sinners living forgiven lives in which the sacraments play an essential part. McAdoo perhaps captures the essential traits of Patrick when he writes:

In his works there clearly emerges the traditional Anglican-ism, conscious of the corporate aspect, historically-minded, conservative as to formularies, liberal in its attitude to contemporary advances, confident of its doctrinal presup-positions, but with a certain insularity which became a general outlook.[23]

11

'Covenant Begun and Continued'

Herbert Thorndike (1598–1672)

I was lucky enough – or perhaps unlucky – to have attended a school with a strong legal tradition. The rogues' gallery in the school hall was full of the names, portraits and photographs of big Scottish legal names. Even the architecture of the school, an early nineteenth-century Age of Reason edifice, expressed the neat and precise language of the lawyers at their best. Arguments and discussions formed an important part of our education.

One important attitude to life which lawyers can helpfully bring to their environment is the way in which human institutions, whether families or corporate bodies, flourish or die by the nature and quality of the *agreements* that create and sustain their lives. All relationships are based on agreements. Friendships grow from mutual affection and respect for boundaries. Good professional relationships need to be nurtured not just on the basis of what one party expects from another, but on the extent to which we are prepared to give some leeway to each other's weaknesses. The increasing atmosphere nowadays of litigation – for many of us a new development, and not always a healthy one – can bring into the forum of official enquiry many matters that a previous age (at its worst) swept under the carpet, or (at its best) simply gave spontaneous space for mutual manoeuvre.

The idea of the agreement, or the contract, lies deep in

human history and therefore in the religions of humanity. If we need to subsist as a community through agreements and contracts, then we are bound to bring such a perspective into the arena of religious faith. All words and terminology have their limitations. 'Agreement' suggests a conversation that is subsequently recorded, and 'contract' has overtones of much detail. The word 'covenant', by contrast, spans these two worlds of verbal conversation and documented detail. In medieval English, a covenant was taken to be a mutual agreement between two or more persons to do or refrain from doing certain acts, with sometimes an undertaking by one of the parties.

It is this bilateral relationship that underlies the covenant as understood in the Old Testament when God calls Noah into the Ark with his family, with two of every living creature, and declares that he will establish a covenant with him (Gen. 6:18). The notion of covenant, the relationship between God and Israel, runs right through the Old Testament.[1] The main tension with which the people of Israel wrestled was the extent to which their calling as God's people was an exclusive one, and how far they would themselves be forgiven.

These are exactly the issues with which the Christian Church has wrestled. How can the Christian gospel, the structures of the Church, and the way that the Church communicates its message and celebrates the sacraments, find the right balance between proclaiming the great and distant and awesome God on high, while at the same time making known the God who is beside us, our companion by the way?

We have seen the use of the word 'covenant' with varying degrees of intensity among the writers that we have looked at so far. Charles Miller has recently described the close relationship between baptism and covenant as 'a theological common place' of this age.[2] We have also observed slight differences of emphasis on precisely those areas which concerned Israel of old: namely, who should be baptized, and to what extent are we forgiven?

The notion of covenant almost took on a life of its own in the next century in the teaching of John Wesley, who was himself strongly influenced by this biblical motif and its seventeenth-century eclipse. For on 25 December 1747, he urged Methodists to renew their covenant with God. He was so captivated by this truth that he held a Covenant Service in the French Church at Spitalfield on 11 August 1755. Since that time, Methodists have held Covenant Services at the start of the calendar year.[3] Many reasons can be offered for this innovation. Perhaps Wesley saw the renewal of covenant as a way of spot-lighting the whole of Christian life, in baptism, Eucharist, and daily living, from a fresh perspective altogether. The ecumenical movement in recent years has enabled this spirituality to be shared among other Christians. The actual form of covenant said nowadays by the whole congregation is a telling reminder of the fact that the covenant of grace which is celebrated at the font and renewed at the Lord's Table only makes sense when it is also allowed to spread across the whole of the Christian life, like butter over a large open sandwich.

> I am no longer my own, but yours.
> Put me to what you will, rank me with whom you will;
> Put me to doing, put me to suffering;
> Let me be employed for you, or laid aside for you,
> Exalted for you or brought low for you;
> Let me be full, let me be empty;
> Let me have all things, let me have nothing;
> I freely and whole-heartedly yield all things to your pleasure and disposal.
> And now, glorious and blessed God, Father, Son and Holy Spirit,
> You are mine and I am yours.

So be it.
And the Covenant now made on earth, let it be ratified
  in heaven. Amen.[4]

Of all the writers we have so far encountered, to none of
them might these rich images be more like music in the ears
than to Herbert Thorndike, perhaps the most prophetic of
all the writers we have so far seen.

We do not know a great deal about Thorndike's early life.[5] He
studied at Trinity College, Cambridge, graduating in 1620. A
brilliant scholar, he became a Major Fellow and was made
Deputy Orator of the University. In that capacity, he preached
the afternoon sermon before the University on the day of
King James I's funeral, 7 May 1626, and the young John
Milton came to hear him.[6] He counted George Herbert among
his friends and held parochial posts, first at Claybrooke, Leic-
ester, in 1639, and then, in 1642, at Barley, which con-
veniently placed him fifteen miles from Cambridge. From here
he was able to continue his association with Trinity College,
where he was Senior Bursar of the College and Lecturer in
Hebrew in the University.

  In 1641 he published his first major work, on primitive
church order.[7] In this book Thorndike argued strongly for a
Church of England reformed on the model of antiquity. It is
something of a paradox to imagine this book's publication
as the Civil War began. Parliament is at war with the King, the
strong Puritan elements are shortly to combine to overthrow
episcopacy and replace it with a Presbyterian ordering of the
church. And here is Thorndike, arguing for the old episcopal
order, but stripped of much of the outward array of church
government that the Puritans themselves disliked so much.
This is one of the books that persuaded Simon Patrick to be
ordained by a bishop.[8]

  Thorndike suffered for his published views. The Parliamen-

tarians deprived him of his living in 1643 and of his Fellowship at Cambridge in 1646. He was able to use his knowledge
of oriental languages when he contributed the Syriac portion
to Brian Walton's Polyglot Bible, which appeared in 1657.
But he did not manage to keep his head down for the entire
Commonwealth period. Life became more difficult for him
after Oliver Cromwell's death and we find him for a short
time in Utrecht in 1659, in the company of Michael
Honeywood, another former Leicestershire incumbent, who
was to become Dean of Lincoln at the Restoration. The Restoration marked a predictable change in Thorndike's fortunes
as well. He was restored to his living at Barley, and also made
a Prebendary of Westminster in 1661, under the new Dean,
John Earle, who with his new colleagues was to bring a new
lease of life to that place.

Among the improvements made to the Abbey was the font,
which was placed on a flight of steps in the western aisle of
the north transept. This positioned it near the north transept
door, making an architectural statement about baptism as
the entrance to the Christian Church. (It was moved to the
west end early in the nineteenth century, when the west door
became the main entrance.) Thorndike may well have been
associated with the procuring of this new font. At any rate,
his name lives on in the baptism register, which reads as
follows: '18th April 1663, Paul Thorndyke, a young man
about twenty years of age, and Duell Pead, one of the King's
scholars, about sixteen years of age, was baptized by the Dean
publickly in the font then newly set up.'[9] Paul Thorndyke
was Herbert's nephew.

Use will doubtless have been made on this occasion of the
new baptism order for those 'of riper years' which was
included in the Prayer Book for the first time in 1662. Thorndike had been present at the 'Savoy Conference' in 1661,
where Restoration ecclesiastics met with Puritans, including
Richard Baxter, to try to find a way round their liturgical

disagreements. He may have had a hand in negotiating this new provision. At any rate Thorndike's preaching and teaching ministry flourished with the Abbey at this time, and he died in 1672.

Thorndike was indeed a prophetic figure and a prolific writer. In his biography of him, Lacey remarks that 'he remained always discursive, unloading his erudition as the drift of an argument called forth. He saw clearly enough, but he saw too many things at once.' And later on he remarks, 'Thorndike never knew when he had said enough.'[10] In addition to the several volumes of published works, there are large boxes of unpublished discourses and sermons in the Muniment Room of Westminster Abbey. The seventeenth-century divines have yet more to teach us.

Thorndike's baptismal priorities are evidenced in the unpublished works. There are two sermons on the baptism of Christ (one on Matthew 3:16–17, the other on Luke 3:21–2).[11] Like Andrewes and Taylor before him,[12] Thorndike sees the baptism of Christ almost as an icon of our own baptism, a foundation narrative for baptism itself. Moreover, there are no fewer than six sermons on the command to baptize all nations at the end of Matthew's Gospel (Matt. 28:19–20).[13] The reader is struck by the sense of a preacher simply pouring out his covenant theology, fervent in the grace of God, the life of that Trinitarian Godhead in humanity, and our response in faith. In the first of these sermons, we come across a characteristic Thorndike rhetorical flourish: 'What cleansing of sin, without baptism in the name of the Father, Son and Holy Ghost? What baptism without believing in the name in which we are baptized? What belief without glorifying the Trinity for God, in the name whereof we believers are baptized?'[14] Thorndike's vision of baptism in terms of cleansing, believing, and glorifying has a wonderfully wholesome ring to it.

The same overall sense of the relentless grace of God is

expressed in one of his unpublished discourses.[15] Here are its opening words:

> The necessity of the sacraments of baptism and of the Eucharist unto salvation consisteth in the Covenant of Grace in which our Salvation consisteth; and which the one of them seteth and inacteth, the other reneweth and replenisheth. It is not the washing of the Body in Baptisme, but the profession of Christianitie made with a good conscience, which saveth us said St Peter (I Peter 3:21).

Thorndike then goes on in this discourse to defend the baptism of children on the basis of the free gift of divine grace. He goes so far as to justify the communion of baptized infants on the basis of juxtaposing Jesus' statement to Nicodemus that one cannot enter the Kingdom of God unless one is born of water and the Spirit (John 3:5) with his assertion that unless we eat the flesh of the Son of Man and drink his blood we have no life in us (John 6:53):

> We must by no means grant, that the church acknowledgeth it an error in doctrine or a sacriledge in profaning the Sacrament to give the Eucharist to Infants . . . for as they who receive the Eucharist are to examine themselves; so they who are to be baptized are to be Christ's disciples.

Thorndike then discusses baptismal practice and deplores the Puritan destruction of medieval fonts, at the same time extolling the custom of using much water – and all within the covenant of grace, of baptism itself.

> Of those whose Sacriledge caused them to destroy the Fonts of Baptisme in our churches, some would have no Christning, but in basins, others but in rivers. And they that make noe account of the ground of Salvation in our

Baptisme, the profession of Christianitie should make sure account of that which saveth not, the washing of the flesh as to voide the Sacraments for want of it, is no great merit. For what is all mistaken Religion but superstition? And what is Superstition but standing upon that, for the service of God, which indeed is not his service. This Church hath nothing to doe without either of both; not allowing sprinkling but in case of necessitie. As not thincking life everlasting to come by taking away or indangering the present. They that have the order thereof agree with itselfe but so limit the sprinkling which the Catechisme alloweth. That which is to be blamed is the neglect of the order which we now acknowledge.

Thorndike's style can hardly be ranked with the clarity of Perkins or the simplicity of Patrick. Sadly, we cannot date these unpublished works, though perhaps the discourse may have been written during the Commonwealth era, which would explain the defensiveness of his attack on those who baptize in basins and use little water. His championing of infant communion, based on his knowledge of the patristic era, is a pointer to future paths. His most vivid picture is of the covenant of grace energizing the people of God in the cleansing waters of baptism, and the profession of the Christian faith in the worship of the Trinity.

Thorndike's longest and probably greatest work was published early in 1659, on the eve of the Restoration. Its title suggests exactly where the Church of England was at that time, namely poised between an era where things were not working out properly, and before another one, in which change was in the air. Into it Thorndike poured all his acute powers of observation, his considerable reading of the Fathers, and the vision for a church reformed along primitive lines. None of these priorities was new to his writings but this particular work gives them the fullest expression. We have seen already that Thorndike was long-winded and his long-windedness is to be found in the title:

> *An Epilogue to the Tragedy of the Church of England being a Necessary Consideration and a Brief Resolution of the Chief Controversies in Religion that Divide the Western Church; Occasioned by the Present Calamity of the Church of England in Three Books, viz. of:*
> I *Principles of Christian Truth*
> II *The Covenant of Grace*
> III *The Laws of the Church.*[16]

It was not received with universal praise by any means. Thorndike had already been deprived by the Parliamentarians of both his living and his Cambridge Fellowship and it was known that he found Puritan worship, particularly preaching, a test of endurance. But an indication of how the Royalist element viewed the work is suggested by the following reaction of Sir Edward Hyde (later Lord Clarendon):

> I pray tell me, what melancholy hath possessed poor Mr Thorndike . . . ? his name and reputation and learning is too much made use of, to the discountenance of the poor church; and though it might not be in his power to be without some doubt and scruples; I do not know what impulsion of conscience there could be to publish those doubts to the world at a time when he might reasonably believe the worse use would be made, and the greatest scandal proceed from them.[17]

This reaction suggests that Thorndike was ahead of his time in viewing the primitive church as a model whereby the Church of England of his time could be re-appraised. Many of the other writers we have looked at so far have based their views (and their part in controversies) on the Early Fathers. But none of them has gone so far as Thorndike in regarding the primitive church as such a paradigm. Indeed, unfavourable reaction to this work may have been the reason for his stay in Utrecht, Holland, in that year.

It is in the second part, *The Covenant of Grace*, that Thorndike discusses baptism in most detail. He begins by outlining three main problems associated with particular distortions of the Christian faith.[18] The first is that baptism is a mere ceremony and is therefore not really necessary; this view he ascribes to the Socinians. To them he asserts that baptism is necessary and that it actually does something. Secondly, there are people who would hold that only those who are predestined by God to be in the covenant should be baptized; Thorndike attacks them for their exclusiveness, and their distortion of the covenant as one which denies the forgiving love of God. Thirdly, there are those who regard themselves as already possessing the Spirit of God, who do not require anything else, and for whom a good life is sufficient in itself; these Thorndike labels Antinomians, and he openly refers to 'all our Anabaptists, all our Familists, all our Enthusiasts and Quakers; all Sectaries whatsoever [who] do believe themselves possessed of the Spirit . . .'[19] These Thorndike regards as inadequate and wrong.

He then treats baptism in terms of its *origin*.[20] He begins boldly: 'the Sacrament of Baptism is that condition which The Covenant of Grace requireth to qualify us for the promises which he tendereth'. This foundational scriptural reference is 1 Peter 3:20–1, that baptism saves, a text which Patrick also uses. 'If Baptism import the condition of The Covenant of Grace which saveth us, our justification may necessarily be wrapt up in the same packet, though to justify and save be several conceits.' For him the 'appeal to a good conscience' of that text refers to the profession of faith in the baptismal liturgy, and the water of baptism 'signifies the temptations of this world, out of which we escape by the means of that sacrament'. For Thorndike, baptism of water and baptism of the Holy Spirit are not in opposition but part of the same sacramental process, which is something of a contrast to Perkins' distinction between the inward and the outward baptism. Thorndike's biblical image of baptism is a strong one, 'a corporation founded for the maintenance and exercise of that Christianity, to which we engage ourselves by baptism'. Baptism, too, is a promise of the future. In discussing that key text on which he preached those seven sermons on the command to baptize at the end of Matthew's gospel (Matt. 28:19), he interprets 'disciples' as those who will take up their cross to follow Christ. Once again, we see here the same emphasis on engagement with the Christian life that we saw in Taylor, Baxter and Patrick. He loves the scene of Jesus and Nicodemus (John 3), soon to be incorporated (in 1662) into the new form of baptism for those 'of riper years' as the scripture passage.[21] For Thorndike the *waters* of baptism signify the work of the Holy Spirit: 'seeing then that the gift of the Holy Ghost depends on the water of baptism, it is manifest, that the cleansing virtue of God's Spirit, in the new birth of sinners, comes not to affect without the same.' We may take this to imply support for the blessing of the water in the baptismal liturgy.

Secondly, Thorndike discusses the nature of the covenant itself.[22] He contrasts the Old Testament with the New Testament. In the former, the children of Israel entered the covenant at circumcision and they were baptized as they passed through a sea, 'under the cloud' without a drop of water to wet them. But the old and the new are different, just as 'the Kingdom of Heaven and the land of promise' are distinct. Baptism is our way of showing that 'the engagement of the second covenant being inepted [begun] and settled upon us by the sacrament of baptism, the promises of The Covenant must needs depends on the same'.

He walks carefully – like Patrick – along the tightrope of making this covenant so demanding as to be impossible to live by, and so undemanding as to be of no substance. 'Now every Covenant, every contract whatsoever, is a law, which the parties interchangeably tie themselves to, being free before; neither can it be a covenant, that imposeth nothing upon one of the parties.' He finds his way through this issue by stressing not the *obligation* so much as the *attractiveness* of the promises of God: 'if all that is said in the Bible of the Second and New Testament or Covenant of Grace, imported no more but a mere promise, was mankind so void of reason as to need all this to persuade him to embrace his own happiness tendered without any reputed disadvantage?'

Fourthly, Thorndike discusses an aspect dear to his heart and not brought out fully by any of the writers we have so far seen – the catechumenate.[23] He is charmed by such a patristic vision of the Church in which catechises is part of its whole life. For Thorndike 'the custom of catechizing' seems to be almost of the essence of the Church. The early writers enable him to see the Eucharist in two parts, the liturgy of the catechumens and the liturgy of the faithful, for the latter of which the catechumens were dismissed. This division was for a reason: 'for it is visible, that the time of any man's continuing *catechumenus* or probationer in Christianity, was required upon no other ground, nor to any other purpose, but that the Church might be reasonably or legally ... assured, that the party pretending to baptism is really resolved to stand to that, which Christianity should require at his hands'. Thorndike would like to revive this vision of the Church, and even include an order of penitents also, those temporarily excluded from communion for grievous sin to the community. Many of his contemporaries place comparable stress on catechesis. We have seen it in several of our writers. Thorndike was therefore not alone; but perhaps more than any of the others, he undergirded it with the practice of the primitive church, in a creative rather than an anachronistic manner. Here is another use of tradition that is thoroughly Anglican.

Again and again, Thorndike emphasizes the *cross* of Christ. He refuses to accept that unbaptized infants go to hell; after all, some early Christians were martyred before they could be baptized. With his vision of the catechizing Church comes also the importance of the outward ceremonies of baptism; and here he refers to the controversy between Hooker and Cartwright.[24] He mentions the white robes after baptism, and the signing of the cross, and he favours strongly the practice of sponsors who 'were no counterfeits, but would stand to what they undertook'. He approves, too, of the practice of penance. But he wisely observes that rigorism leads to greater rigorism.

This part of the discussion is concluded by drawing attention to the teaching of the Prayer Book – still proscribed at the time – about baptism, namely renunciation of evil, the importance of godparents and their relationship with the growing infant, and spiritual rebirth. 'All this can leave no doubt of the communion of the Church of England with the whole Church in this point, so nearly concerning the salvation of all Christians.'

In the next section, Thorndike addresses himself to a number of important pastoral issues.[25] The Baptism of Christ as narrated in the Gospels 'pre-supposeth Repentance'. He winds himself into a recapitulation of some of his previous points, attacking indifference, stressing sacramental efficacy, and holding before him and his readers a vision of a Church in which affection is indeed balanced by demand.[26] Fed by his reading of the Fathers, he discusses the ancient practices of the laying on of hands and signing of the cross, and how these find expression in the sacrament of baptism; and he is familiar, too, with the custom of anointing with chrism at confirmation, which he appears to endorse. He is wedded to confirmation, which he sees as the confirmation of baptism, through the profession of faith of the person being confirmed, and the blessing given by the Church. Because he championed communion of the very young, he presumably favoured early confirmation, like Taylor.[27]

Thorndike is probably the most enigmatic of the writers we have looked at so far. More than any of them, he stands slightly detached from the Church of his time, looking back through an historical telescope to the Fathers with all his enthusiasm to reform the Church of England along primitive lines. But he is still very much rooted in the Reformation era. As Paul Avis has remarked, 'in the final analysis, perhaps, Thorndike, for all his Catholic hedging around of Christian truths, is not so far from that evangelical and christological centre that the Reformers saw as constituting the Church'.[28] His vision of the covenant of grace builds on much of what we have so far seen. Even more than Perkins, Thorndike sees the covenant as a theological tool with which to understand the whole nature of the Church. God takes the initiative, and we respond. God keeps taking the initiative, when our response is weak – as it necessarily is. God lays obligations upon us, and we respond by laying upon ourselves the living-out of the Christian gospel, in all its unpredictabilities. Thorndike's stress on freewill and the human faculties of reason and imagination – not features of Perkins' teaching – lead him to see that the covenant of grace is fed by the continuing work of the Church in catechizing not only infants and the young but the whole people of God. He can be lumberingly repetitive; that is often the style of the prophet. For whereas Patrick is steadfastly loyal to the Prayer Book inheritance, Thorndike has a wider vision of a Prayer Book Church more deeply Reformed and more profoundly Patristic.

Thorndike's view of the covenant of grace is not of a legal document that is signed, but of a vision in which we are caught up, almost an icon. Like Andrewes and Taylor, for him the narrative of Christ's baptism is of paramount importance to his whole scheme. Here, then are the opening words of a sermon preached on Luke's account of the central mystery at Epiphany, surely its Eastern point of origin:

> The Festival of the Epiphany, that is the manifestation of Christ Jesus in our flesh, in the Glory of his God-head, the most Glorious manifestation of it is this, at his baptism. For the nature, honour and Glory of his Father so appeared, when a voice was brought from the most excellent Glory, saying 'thou art my beloved Son in whom I am well pleased'.[29]

12

Retrospect

Thus I was led to consider the meaning of this ordinance of Baptism as a key to the nature of ordinances generally . . . in this way there rose up before me the idea of a Church Universal, not built upon human inventions or human faith, but upon the union which He has formed with his creatures . . .[1]

Whenever I read those words of F. D. Maurice, I have before me a whole series of pictures of the many baptisms at which I presided while I was a parish priest. I can remember a young convert from Islam who insisted on lashings of water being poured over him at the service when he was baptized, confirmed and received communion. The best that we could do in the University Chaplaincy was to set up a paddling pool, decorate the outside with flowers, get him to kneel down inside it, and have a bucket of water poured over his whole body. I can remember baptizing a young girl who loved symbolism and who brought her favourite perfume – at my suggestion – with which to be anointed at the service. I can remember standing at an old font in a medieval church with six squawking babies waiting to be baptized during (lightly filleted) Prayer Book Matins. I can remember, too, a beautifully ordered baptism or two at the Sung Eucharist in another parish church nearby, where extended family and friends joined the local congregation in support and prayer and fellowship around font and altar.

It is so easy to form opinions and make judgements about the effectiveness of this or that service, but I always end up by looking deep within myself and wonder how *faithful* I am to my own baptism. Those telling words of St Augustine – 'I myself cannot grasp the totality of what I am'[2] – spring to mind.

But that is only one side of the coin. Unlike the Eucharist, baptism is not repeated. The Eucharist *is* repeated. We will never fully understand baptism, because it is impossible to express all its potential in one set of experiences, however rich, in one service, however, all-embracing, or in one theological treatise, however eloquent. The Eucharist, on the other hand, is repeated in such a way that one celebration leads into another. Whilst we cannot look too closely for 'results' in what the Eucharist can do, we can nevertheless draw it ever closer to the concerns that we have on particular occasions. It is important to see this essential difference between the two dominical sacraments. Baptism is the beginning and the Eucharist is the repeated continuation of the Christian life in sacramental terms. This is, after all, what Hooker himself means when at the start of his discussion of the Eucharist he asserts that 'the grace which we have by the Holy Eucharist doth not begin but continue life'.[3]

All our writers *burned* with a deep and lasting conviction about the centrality of baptism not only in the worship of the Church but in the life of the Christian. It was not for nothing that Perkins wrote so eloquently, 'if a man would be a student of divinity let him learn and practise his baptism'.[4] Perhaps our writers understood better than many that in the life of faith we can make no assumptions about what people may regard as important to them. The task of theology, therefore, is to reflect anew and afresh on the experience that people have of that life of faith and take the risk of doing so in the shifting sands of changing terminology, liturgical innovation, and even social revolution. But before we look at the particular liturgical and theological issues which they raise, it is perhaps appropriate first to glance at each one of them in turn, for their own particular emphases.

William Perkins gives a vivid portrayal of baptism, strongly based on the Pauline image of dying and rising (Rom. 6:3–11).[5] He sees inward and outward baptism in separate terms, which enables him to retain infant baptism, provided the parents are practising believers; and he has no time for traditional confirmation. A sacrament is not absolutely necessary, but it is a 'prop and stay for faith to lean upon'.[6] He is content with either dipping or sprinkling of water, but implies no liturgical blessing of the water, which would be in line with his own Puritan sympathies. For him, confirmation is a personal testimony by the believer, not a rite of the Church performed by the bishop. From Perkins we gain a picture of a church which is gathered, devoted, well instructed, and constantly challenged. The contrast between inward and outward baptism can be lived with there.

Richard Hooker, on the other hand, opts for a more slanted treatment of baptism. When he writes that 'participation is that mutual inward hold which Christ hath of us and we have of him'[7] he is implying that the inward and the outward are not to be seen in the contrasting way of Perkins. The sacraments are not our own actions, but those of the Holy Spirit. Hooker has a higher doctrine of nature than Perkins, and whilst he is happy to regard certain aspects of the services of the Church as 'accessory', the basic core of the rite and its meaning are not negotiable. When he describes baptism as 'an action in part moral, and in part ecclesiastical, and in part mystical'[8] he is saying something trenchant. Baptism is about lifestyle, it is about liturgy, it is about our sharing in the life of God. And that is why he is so keen on the sign of the cross as awakening the memory – along the lines reminiscent of Augustine's *Confessions* – of the community as it constantly remembers and celebrates the central act of salvation.

Lancelot Andrewes takes a different approach, though the result is similar. Unlike Perkins the popularizer, and Hooker the writer of the definitive treatise, he preaches a sermon which seems like a mixture of gazing at an icon and reading a Shakespeare play. There is an essentially narrative quality to his approach. The icon is the baptism of Christ, and the play is a structured narrative, interspersed with different subsections intended to provide contrast, and even light diversion here and there. Luke's version of the baptism of Christ (Luke 3:21–2) is milked for everything it can give. All the people are being baptized, which means the whole people of God are involved. Jesus prays, thus placing baptism in the context of people coming forward to ask for it, and to pray for it in a liturgy – a scene which provides Andrewes with one of his favourite homiletic mannerisms near the start of his sermons, namely mention of the Trinity – 'the Son in the water, the Holy Ghost in the dove, the Father in the voice'.[9] All through this sermon, Andrewes hammers home his theme that Christ's baptism is *our* baptism, and he takes care to ensure that it is a baptism not only in the Jordan but also into the cross.[10] The Spirit appears in *bodily form* as a dove, as the power and the substance of the gift of the Spirit on those who are baptized. Baptism is about the 'embodied' character of the human race.

George Herbert, by contrast, provides a more straightforward route. In his *Priest To The Temple* the parson is a central figure who approaches the sacrament of baptism with thoughtfulness and reverence. It is a public occasion, not a private one. It is not a human act but the act of God himself, hence the need to give thanks to God for calling us to the knowledge of his grace. The signing of the cross is an essential part of the service, no mere adjunct, which is a point forcibly made in his rebuttal of the Scots Reformer, Andrew Melville.

Baptism is to be remembered. It is a celebration of the prevenient grace of God, as the poems in *The Temple* show all
too clearly: 'you taught the book of life my name . . .'[11]

In John Bramhall, we have a short case-study in what happens to the unbaptized. With energy and clarity, he distinguishes between those who are unable to have their children
baptized and those who neglect the opportunity. So much for
the varieties of human motivation. Secondly, like our other
writers he distinguishes between the visible sign and the
invisible grace. In other words, he refuses to lock God up
into the categories of what the Church does. Then he goes
so far as to suggest that God's grace may work more freely
among unbaptized infants (who are not baptized through
no fault of their own), than among unbaptized adults
(who presumably had the opportunity to do something
about it).[12]

Jeremy Taylor, unlike Bramhall who was in exile on the
Continent during the Commonwealth, lived in forced seclu-
sion at home and used the opportunity to write at considerable length. *Holy Living* yields a prayer for the anniversary
of one's baptism (or birth), which takes us into an effusive
and long-winded world in which the providence and forgiveness of God provide the chance for continued growth in the
life of baptism.[13] But it is in *The Great Exemplar* that we
encounter Taylor's penetrating style. Baptism is first viewed
in its historical context, almost with a touch of what we
would nowadays call comparative religion. Like Andrewes,
he starts with Christ's baptism, but this time in the version
given in Matthew's Gospel (Matt. 3:13-17). Baptism is therefore above all the gift of the Holy Spirit, which 'does only
antedate the work of man'.[14] Baptism is indeed a sacrament
of forgiveness but it does not forgive the sins of the future in
such a way that we do not need to try to live a holy life. And
in the strenuous defence of infant baptism, he seems to hit
an important theological nail on the head when he contends

that 'the church gives the sacrament, God gives the grace of the sacrament'.[15]

Richard Baxter takes us into the Puritan strand of Anglicanism and provides his own liturgy where the faith of the parents is central. The purpose of baptism is to solemnize the covenant of Christianity between God and man, which obliges us to follow Christ as his disciples. He defends the use of water in experiential terms: 'a soul in flesh is apt to use sense, and needs have health of it'. Children of unfaithful parents are not baptized. He has no time for episcopal confirmation, not least because of his own experiences in a churchyard as a teenager, but like Perkins he wants to have an occasion when the conscious believer can own the covenant of grace.[16]

In Simon Patrick we have a different figure altogether. In his first published work, the *Aqua Genitalis*, a more all-embracing view of baptism comes across. Repentance and amendment of life take precedence over innocence and unerring obedience. The profession of faith is more than simply owning the baptismal vows. It is a life of holiness and obedience, grounded in the Trinity. 'We have now relation likewise to Christ as our head, and to the Holy Ghost as the giver of life and grace.'[17] And there are hints at Prayer Book practice, such as godparents, and acquaintance with traditional symbols, such as the use of oil.

Finally, Herbert Thorndike addresses critics perhaps more forcefully than anyone else. Baptism is more than a mere ceremony; it brings us into a relationship with God. Baptism is not just for the supposedly predestined and elect. We *all* need baptism. There is no such thing as an adequate Christianity that relies entirely on people's feelings.[18] There can be no separation of the bodily from the spiritual: baptism of water and the Spirit are one and the same. The baptismal water moreover is a vehicle of God's redemption. Thorndike's vision of the Church is of a community where catechesis – as of old – is not an optional extra but the basis of its life.

And like Andrewes and Taylor, he basks in the narrative of
Christ baptized in the Jordan.

But what of the relationship between our writers and the
liturgy and worship of the Church? Each one of them, with
the exception of Bramhall, refers to the liturgy as the locus
and expression of the Church's teaching. We have seen many
examples of this, whether in Hooker dealing systematically
with controversial practices such as the sign of the cross, or
in Taylor's implicit assumption that Jesus by 'blessing' the
Jordan also blesses the baptismal waters.

Each one of them holds in the background the Prayer Book
services, whether for exposition, comment, or criticism.[19] It
begins with a short exhortation which alludes to rebirth (John
3:5), and continues with a prayer based on that of Martin
Luther, using different motifs of water in the Old Testament,
and rejoicing in the salvation wrought by Christ in the
Church. Then follows the prayer for the person to be baptized
about knocking at the door and entering the Kingdom of
Heaven.[20] Jesus taking the children into his arms and blessing
them (Mark 10:13–16) is the reading, which is followed by
an exhortation, which interprets it – a passage increasingly
significant as objectors to infant baptism become more vocif-
erous. A further prayer for the baptism candidate introduces
a short exhortation to the godparents; this forms a natural
transition to the renunciation of evil and the profession of
faith, which uses the Apostles' Creed in its interrogatory form.
More prayers for the infants in their future life of grace follow, leading into the blessing of the water, and the baptism
itself. The signing of the cross takes place immediately afterwards and the service concludes with the Lord's Prayer, a
prayer of thanksgiving, and an exhortation to the parents
and godparents.

How is this inheritance affected by our writers and their
colleagues? We have already mentioned the 1604 Canons,

which forbid parents to serve as godparents, and which defend 'the lawful use of the cross in baptism'.[21] The reasons given there reflect the views and language of Richard Hooker himself; the cross is central to the Christian faith, we are not to be ashamed of it, and we must not refrain from using it just because others (i.e. Roman Catholics) abuse it. Furthermore, we have observed the influence of Perkins on the 'Directory' rite which was produced by the Westminster Assembly, where baptism was debated in July, August and October of 1644. Agreement was reached that baptism must be held in church, the child brought in its parents' arms, and a balance maintained in the service over inward versus outward baptism.[22]

When it comes to the 1662 Prayer Book, there are a number of significant enrichments to the 1552 service.[23] The number of godparents is specified exactly as in the Middle Ages, namely three in all, and two of the gender of the child. The priest *must* start the service at the font, which is to be filled with pure water. The exhortation before the profession of faith now includes an additional mention of the sanctifying work of the Holy Spirit and expresses the hope that the child will come to Confirmation – two not insignificant additions. Godparents must answer 'in the name of this child', and not simply speak as if they are the child themselves – an important nuance, which stresses their representative character, as standing there on behalf of the whole community. There is a fresh question after the profession of faith, 'Wilt thou then obediently keep God's holy will and commandments, and walk in the same all the days of thy life?' One thinks of Taylor's 'following holy life' and Baxter's emphasis on discipleship.

The prayer over the water is stronger on blessing. The sign of the cross is more explicitly directed, and there is an added rubric at the end which refers the reader to the appropriate Canon of 1604 explaining why the sign of the cross is retained. The entirely new order of baptism for those 'of riper years' has the Nicodemus passage (John 3:1–8) at the point where the infant baptism rite uses Jesus embracing the children in his arms (Mark 10:13–16).

The confirmation rite is similarly enriched. Candidates must profess the Christian faith for themselves, which is in line with several of our writers, especially Perkins and Baxter. The Lord's Prayer is said immediately after the confirmation, the corresponding position in baptism and the Eucharist. There is also an additional prayer at the end, to round off the rite. This was taken from those directed by Cranmer to be used at the altar before the blessing when there is no communion. The prayer the good Archbishop will have known well from the end of Prime, the first Latin daily office of the morning. It expresses the meaning of many of these improvements in 1662, which point to discipleship, holy living, earthing the profession of the Christian faith, and much else that we have read hitherto:

O Almighty Lord, and everlasting God, vouchsafe, we beseech thee, to direct, sanctify, and govern, both our hearts and bodies, in the ways of thy laws, and in the works of thy commandments; that, through thy most mighty protection both here and ever, we may be preserved in body and soul; through our Lord and Saviour Jesus Christ.

What lies behind all these changes? The role of godparents is sharpened. The sign of the cross is defended. The font has a central liturgical place. The water that it contains is now explicitly blessed. All this is grist to the mill of many of our writers. Moreover, confirmation is seen more and more as needful, as the seventeenth century progresses. But the anomaly as to whether confirmation was ever really universally performed remains, for the rubric about admission to communion in 1662 which hitherto restricted access to those who were confirmed has now the eloquent addition 'or be ready and desirous to be confirmed'.

The picture that we gain from these debates and changes is of a church that is trying to adapt itself to new situations, which cannot be explained by the process of mere editorial improvement. The Prayer Book tradition about baptism is not just asserting itself for the sake of doing so in 1662. It is trying to adapt to new circumstances and to answer its critics, most eloquently of all by the alterations in that short exhortation in the baptism service which now includes reference to the sanctifying power of the Holy Spirit and the possibility of the infant coming forward for confirmation as a mature Christian. The concluding prayer, too, in the confirmation service makes the same point: sacraments and sacramental rites are vital for the work of the gospel but so is simple Christian discipleship.

If the liturgical picture is a vibrant and changing one, this is true also of the theological scene. It would be folly to attempt to construct a uniform picture from nine such varied writers. One important point of comparison is the contrasting Bible texts each of them uses for his particular approach or context of writing.

We have already noted Perkins' attachment to the Pauline image of dying and rising with Christ (Rom. 6:3–11). That dramatic image draws into focus the ordinary Christian dying and rising with Christ – hence, in Perkins' case, his concern about the relationship between inward and outward baptism. And Baxter, though markedly different from Perkins, is strongly influenced by Perkins' love of this Pauline image. Hooker's deep and penetrating discussion of participation – sharing in the life of God – is grounded in the view that in baptism the new Christian is reborn of water and Spirit (John 3:5), whereas Lancelot Andrewes, in characteristic vein, paints a scene of heaven opening at the baptism of Christ, in its rich Lucan version (Luke 3:21–2).

It is less easy to pin Herbert down to a biblical text, with his abounding confidence in the providence of God, but perhaps his delightful image of 'the plaister upon the boil' (Isa. 38:21) encapsulates his view of baptism as a sacrament of forgiveness. Taylor is captivated by the baptism of Christ, but in another version from Andrewes (Matt. 3:13–17), and he also uses this passage – uniquely – in his liturgy of baptism. To use Christ's baptism as the foundation for a theology of baptism opens the way for being strong on the work of the Holy Spirit in sanctifying the believer in holy living. Patrick adopts the baptism of the jailer by Paul and Silas (Acts 16:33) as his starting-off point, thereby showing the immediacy and accessibility of baptism, which can in its own good time lead to spiritual growth and deepened profession of the Christian faith. Finally, the loquacious Thorndike loves the command of Christ to his disciples to baptize as a text for several of his sermons (Matt. 28:19–20), and uses the more intricate truth that baptism 'now saves you, not as a removal of dirt from the body but as an appeal to God for clear conscience . . .' (1 Pet. 3:21). For him baptism is an action of God, intended to bring us back to him through Christ. It is interesting to observe that nearly all these scripture texts are *narratives* of one kind or another.

But what of the theological emphases which emerge from our writers? There are a number of themes that they have in common. Covenant is a central motif for Perkins but it is used briefly by Hooker and Andrewes and later on it becomes central to the writings of Taylor, Baxter, Patrick and Thorndike. They all agree on a relationship between baptism and the covenant of grace but there are significant differences. Perkins believes that we are brought into the covenant of grace by being born of Christian parents, whereas Patrick holds that baptism seals that covenant. The beauty of the covenant image is that it is dynamic and non-institutional, so long as legalism does not creep in. Alan Torrance has recently drawn attention to the dangers of this approach in what he calls 'the western order of salvation', where 'law . . . is the necessary presupposition for an awareness of sin, which is the impetus for repentance, through which we may experience God's grace and forgiveness and know the joy of reconciliation'.[24]

Alan Torrance goes on to suggest, in line with Karl Barth, that God's purposes for humanity are filial not legal, covenantal rather than contractual – and by covenantal he means *unconditional*. Here is the heart of the issue of covenant language which Taylor perhaps expresses most positively, but without disallowing the need for holy life:

> In the gospel the covenant was established upon faith and repentance, but it was consigned in baptism, and was verifiable only in the integrity of a following holy life according to the measure of a man; not perfect, but sincere; not faultless, but heartily endeavoured.[25]

All our writers – to a greater or lesser extent – are Trinitarian in their theology. Andrewes, Taylor and Thorndike are off to a good start in the way they turn baptism into an epiphany of the Lord, like the Eastern Fathers. Andrewes has a particularly powerful view of the Trinity and makes a point of working this into his preaching. Patrick links the command of Jesus to the disciples to baptize with the promise that 'I am with you always' (Matt. 29:19–20) and suggests that the promise of Christ's presence is in the sacrament of baptism itself. If Perkins has a Christ-centred piety, perhaps he was restrained in his language about the Holy Spirit, particularly when one compares him with the more exotic outpourings of Taylor. But none of them can quite reach the intensity of Taylor's Trinitarian piety when he prays for the newly baptized in the following terms:

O God be thou his Father forever, Christ his elder Brother and Lord; the Church his Mother, that the Body of Christ be his food, the blood of Christ be his drink and the Spirit the earnest of his inheritance.[26]

Many of these writers draw different strands together in a satisfying manner. For example, when Andrewes links the Jordan baptism with what he calls the 'cross baptism' he is not just referring obliquely to the sign of the cross, he is making a vital connection between the two points of axis that lie at the heart of baptism itself, namely the Christ who comes to bless the waters at Jordan and the Christ who dies on Calvary for our justification. The liturgical truth goes one state further, for it serves to draw together the two cycles of the liturgical year, namely Christmas and Easter.

When it comes to confirmation, our writers differ somewhat. The Puritan strand represented by Perkins and Baxter sees confirmation as a conscious 'owning' of the Christian faith by the mature believer. Hooker, on the other hand, knows his history and regards the laying on of hands by the bishop as an essential part of growing to a mature faith. When Simon Patrick remarks that 'in baptism the Holy Ghost was conveyed as a sanctifier, so herein as a comforter and strengthener' he is meeting the critics of confirmation on theological ground. We are not just confirming because it has always been done or because some people happen to be ready to say something about their Christian faith. There are unresolved tensions here, and Taylor's enthusiasm for early communion as a priest does not mix easily with his enthusiasm for confirmation when he has been made a bishop.

At the end of the day, however, the question must be asked, 'What does baptism actually do?' Whereas the traditional medieval Catholic reply would be that 'baptism washes away original sin', not one of our writers would answer the question in that way. In fact, only three of them mention original sin, namely Perkins, Baxter and Taylor. Instead, each one of them starts his discussion within the context of the saving work of Christ, for the past, the present and the future. The real question is, how *much* does baptism actually do? Perhaps we may be helped from another quarter.

In an earlier chapter, we outlined three Reformation approaches to baptismal theology which looked at baptism in terms of how the symbol of water functions.[27] These were symbolic memorialism, symbolic parallelism, and symbolic instrumentalism. The first looks back to the cross and places a strong emphasis on faithful reception. The second argues for a radical distinction between inward and outward baptism. The third argues that baptism conveys what it signifies. Theological writers – and preachers, too – are quite capable of veering from one to the other. The three views represent a shift from, in the first instance, a radically humanistic view, through a centrist position, to a reformed Catholic one.

How do our writers fare here? None of them falls into the category of symbolic memorialism completely. Perkins, for all that he regards sacraments as a prop to faith, and therefore has memorialist leanings, is at the end of the day a symbolic parallelist. God's action of grace and the Church's care and nurture of her young operate not simultaneously but in parallel. Baxter approaches this position also, as he draws around the infant the faith of the parents and the support of the community and prays fervently for the future.

What of the others? Most of them could be described as symbolic instrumentalists, which should hardly surprise us, in view of the fact that the twenty-seventh of the Thirty-Nine Articles refers, as we shall see, to baptism functioning 'as an instrument'. Hooker and Andrewes are definitely of that view, as are Herbert, Bramhall and Thorndike, with their insistence on the action of the Church by obedience and intention being also an action of God himself. Taylor and Patrick, on the other hand, veer ever so slightly back towards symbolic parallelism, but from a firm starting point of instrumentalism. Taylor, after all, is the one who states that 'the Church gives the sacrament, God gives the grace of the sacrament', and Patrick contends that baptism 'signifies not one thing, but the whole religion; and not only signifies but engages us unto our duty'. Perhaps this only reflects the fact that Taylor and Patrick had a greater interest in what H. R. McAdoo calls 'moral-ascetic theology', namely the applying of the gospel to daily living. But perhaps, too, symbolic instrumentalism does not quite cover the whole picture. We shall return to this matter in the following chapter.

The main changes made in the 1552 Prayer Book baptism service concern what happens immediately after the baptism itself. In 1549, the priest anointed the infant on the head and the accompanying prayer, based closely on the medieval Latin rite, addressed the newly baptized as being now 'regenerate . . . by water and the Holy Ghost'. In 1552, the anointing was abolished and instead the priest addressed the congregation thus: 'Seeing now, dearly beloved brethren, that these children be regenerate and grafted into the body of Christ's congregation; let us give thanks unto God for these benefits and with one accord make our prayers unto Almighty God that they may lead the rest of their life accordingly to this new beginning.'[28]

In this formula we find expressed the all-embracing character of baptism. It is indeed a 'beginning', as Hooker saw so clearly. It does indeed cause the newly baptized to be born again. But it also looks forward to what Taylor would call 'a following holy life', which is to be led 'according to this beginning'.

The same paradox is embedded in the twenty-seventh of the Thirty-Nine Articles of Religion:

Baptism is not only a sign of profession, and mark of difference, whereby Christian men are discerned from others that be not christened, but is also a sign of regeneration or new birth, whereby, as by an instrument, they that receive baptism rightly are grafted into the church; the promises of the forgiveness of sin, and of our adoption to be the sons of God by the Holy Ghost, are visibly signed and sealed; faith is confirmed; and grace increased by virtue of prayer unto God.[29]

This Article dates from 1553, the year after Cranmer's baptism rite takes its definitive form. It incorporates the same teaching and the same balance. There is little in this particular Article with which any of our writers would have quarrelled, with the exception of Perkins and possibly Baxter. It is this same paradox of beginning *versus* the life of discipleship. We are back to the paradox of baptism as both sacrament and experience. But the dangers are apparent of driving a wedge between them, and removing from baptism the pastoral context that our writers saw so clearly as vital for what the Article describes as receiving baptism 'rightly'.

Baptism does indeed do something to the new Christian – even though the effects are not necessarily seen immediately. This takes us deep into the mystery of why God chooses to use sacraments in the first place. Words have to pale into insignificance, however eloquent or precise or beautiful. Indeed, we are back to that simple but profound view of the human race before God enunciated by Simon Patrick:

He admits us into that covenant of grace, which accepts of repentance instead of innocence, and of amendment of life instead of unerring obedience.[30]

Repentance and amendment of life begin at the font – and continue at the Lord's Table.

13

Prospect

The Holy Spirit has a habit of blowing apart 'the best laid schemes of mice and men' – and the diaries of bishops as well. A particular instance saw me and my chaplain suddenly in the north of the diocese at the bedside of a young man who was dying of a brain tumour. Chance had brought him into direct contact with the local priest. He knew that he had not long to live. He asked to be baptized and confirmed.

The prognosis was not good – in fact, I was told that he might not have more than forty-eight hours to live. On arrival at the house, I found the atmosphere in the bedroom tense but expectant. A make-shift altar was prepared and a bowl was made ready with water in it. I looked at him and he looked at me and we gradually warmed to each other as a curious conversation developed, in the course of which he nodded and smiled, and occasionally responded with a few words. I put on my vestments and told him a little bit about each, all the time relating what I was saying to the mystery of baptism. The white alb is the garment of those who put on Christ (Gal. 3:27). The stole is the burden that Christ makes light (Matt. 11:29). The chasuble is the all-embracing love and mercy of God himself (Deut. 33:27). The pectoral cross is the sign in which we are more than conquerors (Rom. 8:37).

As the service began we all slipped into a moment of eternity, where time stood still and where simple actions and gestures were touched by the Holy Spirit. Images fitted in and

out of my mind as I baptized and confirmed him, like dying
and rising with Christ, the washing away of sin, rebirth of
water and the Spirit. When I anointed him with chrism, it
was as much a gesture of healing as of imparting the Mes-
sianic promises of Christ. As we shared the bread and wine,
there was a feeling of being in heaven already, which
reminded me of Taylor's words on the Eucharist, 'nothing
else but the actual enjoying of heaven is above it'.

I do not expect to preside at baptism/confirmation/Euchar-
ists like that every day. It was in any case the most rapid
catechesis that I had ever carried out. But that afternoon's
experience cast all questions of what Richard Hooker calls
'lets and impediments' to the four winds. Here was human
need and here was the Church sharing in that pain and reaching up into the life of God. In the event, the young man lived
for another two months, in which time was measured in depth
rather than length, and when he did die, he left behind him
special gifts, special moments, special blessings. And not one
of us who was there that afternoon will ever be the same
again.

What I have described is a very twentieth-century scene.
But it could have happened at any time and in any place.
Rapid travel made it easier for me than it might have been
when Simon Patrick was Bishop of Ely, or John Bramhall was
Archbishop of Armagh, or Lancelot Andrewes was Bishop of
Winchester. I would hazard a guess that if George Herbert
or Richard Hooker had been faced with a similar request as
parish priests, they would have gone there and then, and
baptized the young man. They would have offered him catechesis – never very much in the circumstances – and given
him the sacrament of Holy Communion on the spot. This is
where the gospel demands are always ready to impinge upon
norms and change them. These demands, moreover, are
always ready to speak of the never-ending love of God. In
one of his many references to the Trinity in the great Whitsun

sermons, Lancelot Andrewes makes bold to preach in unashamedly aquatic terms:

> The Father, the Fountain; the Son, the Cistern; the Holy Ghost, the Conduit-pipe, or pipes, rather (for they are many) by and through which they are derived down to us . . .[1]

We have indeed seen a varied picture thus far. We have watched nine writers labouring with unbounded enthusiasm in the business of *interpreting* the sacrament of entry into the Church to a confused and confusing world. We have seen the medieval inheritance in the form of infant baptism, followed by catechism, followed (ideally) by confirmation at the hands of the bishop, followed by Holy Communion. We have also seen the signs of this scheme already breaking down, as witness the many bishops who did not manage to confirm in their dioceses, and the Puritan-minded clergy who did not themselves believe in that additional sacramental rite in any case. We have seen, too, the emergence in the 1662 Prayer Book of the form for the baptism of those of 'riper years', with all the pastoral overtones that this new rite expressed, namely believing adults who either could not be or were not baptized as infants. What a telling picture that the Bible reading for the office of the baptism of infants should have been Jesus blessing the children (Mark 10:13–16), whereas those baptized who were of 'riper years' heard the narrative of Jesus addressing Nicodemus (John 3:1–8) – both of them much-used texts, but the latter perhaps the most popular at the time for defending baptism.

In our own time, however, we have witnessed the further breakdown of this scheme. We have provision for the baptism, confirmation and first communion at one and the same service of adult candidates, alongside infant baptism, followed by confirmation preparation, followed by communion at the confirmation Eucharist. But, there is also a third 'route', which is characterized by people lapsing from baptized – and even confirmed – Christian membership, and wanting to ritualize their return to the fold after a powerful conversion experience; and one may also add those who want to be received from other churches.[2] Our writers would all respond by insisting on the unrepeatability of baptism. A spate of new rites surrounding baptism has indeed developed in all the major Western churches, Anglican included. These often include a full catechumenate.[3] Many churches have at the same time slipped into using the term 'initiation' in an often imprecise manner, following the lead taken by social anthropologists earlier this century.[4] Such a change in nomenclature suggests that baptism cannot really be pinned down, an important truth in itself, though whether the use of the term 'initiation' does not in fact serve in the end to undermine the centrality of baptism is another matter.

What, then, can our nine writers tell us, who live in an age in which the traditional models of making new Christians have fragmented even further? There are three ways in which they can speak to us.

The first concerns *the relationship between theology and liturgy*. Prayer and belief form a strong cohesive unit in the life of the individual and in the life of the community. When Prosper of Aquitaine (c.390–463) argued for tradition located in worship in the conviction that the 'law of prayer may establish a law of belief', he was saying something profound.[5] The relationship between worship and belief has not always been entirely straightforward. But of all the churches that came out of the tensions of the Reformation, it is the Anglican branch that can lay claim to a special place in this debate, because of the supreme place given to *The Book of Common Prayer* as the doctrinal formulary of the Church.

Not that the Prayer Book remained unchanged – far from it. We have seen both *textual, contextual* and *conceptual* adaptations going on throughout our period. Texts were altered here and there and new material was introduced in 1662. One only has to think of the additions to the prayer over the water, and that expressive concluding prayer in the confirmation rite. Contexts altered, too, as witness the need for a separate form of baptism for those of 'riper years'. It was also necessary to direct how godparents should be selected and to state that the priest should stand at the *font*. These were not to be matters relegated to chance. There is, too, a significant conceptual shift, hence the increasing popularity of the covenant motif in discourse about baptism and confirmation as the seventeenth century progressed, even though that term was only implicit – and never explicit – in the Prayer Book services. In other words, the Prayer Book was being adapted and *re-interpreted*, as is the case on a grander scale in world-wide Anglicanism today.

Here is the Anglican ethos at work on its own terrain. One can be well aware of how much source-material was available then in the production, adaptation and re-interpretation of these liturgical texts, just as today. All our writers knew well the limits of the construction of liturgy and that it is not possible to put every conceivable article of liturgical goods into the Church's shop-window. Choices have to be made. For example, popular as the nuanced covenant–theology of Taylor and others manifestly was, there was no desire to introduce it explicitly into the Prayer Book rite in 1662. Moreover labels are always hard to use accurately. But within the overall framework of the sixteenth- and seventeenth-century European theological scene, all our writers – and many others like them – merit the term 'Reformed Patristic'. They were all sons of the Reformation who loved tradition, and through their (sometimes not uncritical) loyalty to the Prayer Book and their desire to adapt and re-interpret it here and there, they bear witness to this new, living and literary tradition that has eyes open on the past, looks to the present and dreams of the future. The Anglican tradition is one of judicious re-interpretation, and this is where its catholicity is to be found.[6] It is never a straightforward process, but it is a significant – and often undervalued – endemic characteristic that merits recognition on a wider scale.

Moreover, liturgy has its limits, and never more so than in areas of dispute and option. Many of today's rites have a flexibility built into them that meets some of the Puritan objections to the Prayer Book, but which also contributes to a sense of destabilization. For example, the use of oil and the giving of a lighted candle are not mandatory in the *Alternative Service Book* of 1980, and the sign of the cross can take place either before or after the baptism.[7] More importantly, symbolism needs a doctrinal critique, not in order to define it too narrowly, but to give it the context in which it can grow. For example, in the debates about the sign of the cross, many of our writers, particularly Richard Hooker and George Herbert, saw its importance as a secondary – and not a primary – symbol in which it could find its own climate and speak in different ways, as badge, as reminder, and as sign of shame. On the whole, they got the balance right. That may mean that we in our day need to look more imaginatively and theologically at the way the secondary symbolisms of our rites function. For example, oil should smell, it should be really tactile, and it should speak of the healing and salvific character of Christ's work, as well as pointing to our share in the community of Christ. Similarly, a light warms and cleanses and burns – as well as illuminates – the Christian path.[8] At root, our writers would (most of them) beckon us to appreciate the benefits of an ordered liturgy within a literary tradition, imaginatively presented. They would eschew 'ad hoc' texts, as much as woodenness of performance. All this would be in the interests of the law of prayer establishing a law for belief.

The second area concerns *theological imagery*. We have

seen three main biblical images coming through again and
again in our respective writers. There is the Easter image of
dying and rising (Rom. 6:3–11). There is the image of washing (1 Cor. 6:11). There is the image of rebirth in the womb
(John 3:5). In a recent study, Peter Robinson has applied the
insights of anthropology to baptism, using the terminology of
James Fernandez to describe these three motifs as 'organizing
metaphors'.[9] For Fernandez, organizing metaphors are 'the
ones which act both strategically on inchoate subjects and set
a dominant tone for the ritual'.[10] They do not act in a random
manner but rather show an innate coherence to the way in
which, in our case, baptism relates to and re-interprets human
experience. When one looks at baptismal liturgy and theology
across the centuries, these three biblical themes emerge very
much in terms of organizing metaphors, because they inform
and feed theological reflection as well as the writing of
prayers.

Each has its weakness when used on its own, as we have
already seen. Dying and rising with Christ runs the risk of
being weak on the work of the Holy Spirit – as we saw
in Perkins. The washing away of sin, which is noticeably
underplayed in modern rites, Anglican as well as Roman
Catholic, has the fundamental weakness of being retrospec-
tive; we can only be washed once in baptism and yet we keep
committing more sins, and that needs its own explanation.
Not one of our writers uses this theme exclusively or domi-
nantly. A baptismal theology which relies exclusively on
washing must either be very *objective* (baptism washes away
original sin), or very *subjective* ('the inward baptism of washing throughout my life'). The image of rebirth in the Spirit
needs the cross as well, as Andrewes knew full well in his
Whitsun Sermon, and Taylor in his musings about Christian
obedience.

The fact is, of course, that we need all three. The consensus
from our writers, however, is that the foundational metaphor

is that of rebirth, because it most clearly expresses the action of God in Trinity in the human person. (In this, they follow the Prayer Book rite.) This is why, one suspects, the narrative of the baptism of Christ gripped both Andrewes and Taylor and also Thorndike. For it is in the narrative of Christ's baptism that we can see the human story of salvation enacted for us as Christ comes to the Jordan and stands alongside all the people, and is baptized and prays; and heaven opens and the Spirit descends upon him in bodily form as a dove; and a voice comes from heaven declaring him the beloved Son. For in the Jordan narrative we can see, too, the washing away of sin, and the plumbing of the depths. The Gospel narratives of Christ's baptism have fed theology and iconography from the earliest times.[11] But our three writers who enthuse about Christ's baptism regard it as a kind of 'institution narrative' for baptism. In other words, they see the importance of the 'story' of Christ's baptism as a way of expressing our rebirth as God's sons and daughters at the font.

When applying these three organizing metaphors, with rebirth as the central one, to baptismal theology, it is important to reflect upon what baptism actually does. God's unconditional gift of baptism leads into faithful reception. As Oulton wrote some years ago, 'Christian experience seems to show that what the Christian actually receives in baptism, beyond the symbolic seal of membership with Christ, is but the initial impulse of the divine power to start him upon his heavenward way.'[12]

In the previous chapter, we drew attention to the importance of a theology of baptism that reflected upon its symbolic function. 'Symbolic memorialism' can only look back to the cross, and therefore weaken the sacrament itself. 'Symbolic parallelism' – to put it somewhat directly – wants things both ways; in other words, baptism and salvation can float rather too freely from each other. 'Symbolic instrumentalism', on the other hand, stands firmly in the tradition of Augustine and the Fathers in the conviction that baptism does what it is intended to do, namely conveys the gifts of God to the new believer. The effects may take a life-time – but then, this is the very nature of baptism as a beginning rather than a completion. Perhaps this is why 'symbolic relationalism' as a term may be nearer the mark. Divine initiative and human response are held together. A wholesome sacramental theology is about God's action and our faithful reception, for all sacraments have to hold in tension divine initiative and human response – hence, for example, Patrick's carefully crafted approach to the baptismal covenant. 'Symbolic relationalism' itself expresses the sacrament as both *sign* and *instrument.*[13]

Where it is working in the human domain it is strong without being mechanical, and personal without being wholly subjective. In more contemporary terms, it is both 'event' and 'process': hence the importance of the narrative of Christ's baptism, which leads straight into the temptation – a pattern for the Christian life itself, as Taylor saw clearly, particularly in *The Great Exemplar.*

We do, indeed, need the three metaphors. 'Dying and rising with Christ' has perhaps figured too strongly in recent years in the production of new liturgical texts.[14] The image of washing is crucial, but perhaps our writers show that while sin must not be underplayed, too close a connection between baptism and original sin (which most of them avoided) underplays the need for what Taylor called 'holy living' and Patrick called 'a profession of holiness and obedience'. The image of rebirth is the organizing metaphor in which Andrewes, Taylor and Thorndike saw the most complete picture of the fallen and redeemed human race and God in Trinity at work there.

The third area where our writers can help us concerns *specific issues*. Here, we may allow each one of them his own particular slant. Perkins must not be lost in the welter of more confident Anglican writing simply because of his contention that the inward and outward baptisms are so distinct. His is a vital protest against formalism, and his rejection of rebaptism is perhaps the most convincing of all.

Hooker's sense of participating in the life of God must also save us, in the words of T. F. Torrance, 'from regarding baptism *in the flat*'.[15] This leads Torrance to a sceptical view of the ritual act, but it would lead Hooker, on the contrary, to look back to baptism as an event to be remembered and celebrated: hence the importance of its public character, no mere vain ceremony, but an action of God in our midst.

Andrewes' vision of heaven opening underscores the transcendental dimension of baptism. As Andrewes himself points out, it happily undermines what we would today call the 'privatization' of baptism. We do not have to create an atmosphere for this to be seen and felt. But we need a sense of Christ being present at the font, just as he is at the altar. Herbert's stress on providence can only serve to make us think hard before we underplay the role of godparents. He would not approve of God's future being submitted to the modern Filofax. Baptism is not achieved as a result of human effort. It is about the future, offered in trust by the whole community, not just the family.[16] The burning question of what happens to the unbaptized is dealt with succinctly by Bramhall, who draws a sharp distinction between those who are unable to be baptized, and those who do not get there through apathy.

Taylor's focus on holy living is necessarily fed by a strong doctrine of the Holy Spirit, perhaps the strongest we have seen, apart from Andrewes'. This necessarily enables him to ask questions about communicating people rather earlier than may have been fashionable at the time. His enthusiasm for confirmation, once he became a bishop, perhaps draws attention to a debate that is still going on.[17] Baxter, on the other hand, like Perkins before him, will not allow us to regard baptism as the end; hence that prayer immediately after baptism in which we find the words, 'be reconciled to him, and take him for thy child, renew him to the image of thy Son and make him a fellow citizen of the Saints and one of thy house-hold'.

Patrick will never let go of the whole human personality – critical faculties included – being redeemed by the grace of God, and used in his service. And perhaps of all our writers, with the possible exception of Taylor, he begins to view the baptismal water from a perspective that would nowadays be called 'anthropological'. Not for him a mindless Christianity that exalts the non-rational above all else. His openness to the past, as in the use of oil, is a pointer to the future. And Thorndike, for all that he repeats the theme of covenant, will never let it become an exclusive cuckoo in the baptismal nest. Before Thorndike, the gospel is about affection as well as demand. His vision of a catechumenate can only be regarded as prophetic.

There are, however, some open questions. Confirmation is by 1662 a more significant liturgy with a profession of faith by the candidates, and yet the rubric about admission to communion is made less restrictive. One senses that the system did not entirely work. Some of our writers, like Hooker and Thorndike, were aware that confirmation emerged from an uncertain history where the laying on of hands by the bishop took place in various different circumstances. These included reconciling heretics and absolving penitents, in which the gesture was a 'given', but the libretto varied as to the way the Church decided what it was doing. Perhaps they could foresee the wider and more 'extended' use of confirmation that is emerging in some parts of Anglicanism today. All of them, however, were aware that the bishop was the liturgical president of baptism and confirmation in antiquity. Such a view could not be enforced immediately after the Reformation. But it is certainly becoming increasingly common today. In the end we may well ask in the face of such far-seeing seventeenth-century writers, what can we today identify as sparkling truths that may only find their realization in what Michael Ramsey used to call 'the great Christian centuries to come'?

Surrounded by so a great a company of witnesses, a re-orientation towards a baptismal model of the Church begins to become a pressing need.[18] All too often we have heard rhetoric that suggests that the Eucharist makes the Church. In fact, it is Christ who does, first through baptism, and only then through the Eucharist. *Baptism* is the first dominical sacrament and it is to the Jordan that Christ continues to beckon us.

The one writer from a neighbouring tradition who has a great deal in common with much of what we have so far seen is the Danish Lutheran, Nikolai Grundtvig.[19] Of all the figures in the nineteenth-century Roman Catholic and Protestant world, it was Grundtvig above all who preached and wrote hymns – important in the Lutheran tradition – about the centrality of baptism. As Christian Thodberg has shown, Grundtvig singles out many aspects of the baptismal rite for comment in his sermons and for inspiration in his hymns.[20] These include the sign of the cross, Luther's version of the prayer about asking and knocking, the Marcan narrative of Jesus with the children, the renunciations and profession of faith, and the greeting of peace. Much of this appears also in Cranmer's baptismal rite, and in so many of the modern baptismal liturgies. In Grundtvig's hymn on the baptism of Christ, each verse ends with the refrain: 'Here you see over baptism – the door of God's house stands open.'[21]

It is so easy to let baptism degenerate into a social construct, a thing that is 'done', beautifully packaged and defined. But our writers are all the time working *against* that tendency, as they seek to liberate baptism to do its proper task. In our day, however, the fashion for renewing (or reaffirming) baptismal vows on all sorts of occasions is not the way to heed Perkins' challenge that 'the best commentary to a man's own self is his own baptism'.

We have instead to go much deeper. In order to effect this re-orientation, we need good, rich, resonant and theologically powerful liturgies, which are stable and convincing. We also need many more baptismal hymns. We need to bring baptismal resonances right into the Eucharist itself, particularly the eucharistic prayer. We need to place baptism at the heart of our ordination rites. We need a renewed interest in baptismal architecture. We need a revitalized baptismal iconography. We need, above all, a deeper baptismal theology.

All this would be but a small step along the road of appropriating what our writers are calling us to be and do, and letting them inform our own vision in a very different century. Such inspiration as this lies behind the following prayer, which was drafted for the new baptism rite of the Church of England. It is a baptismal prayer, a prayer to bless the water in the name of the Holy Trinity, for All Saints-tide:

Lord of the heavens,
we bless your name for all your servants
who have been a sign of your grace through the ages.

You delivered Noah from the waters of destruction;
you divided the waters of the sea,
and by the hand of Moses
you led your people from slavery
into the promised land.

You made a new covenant in the blood of your Son
that all who confess his name
may, by water and the Spirit,
enter the covenant of grace,
receive a pledge of the kingdom of heaven,
and share in the divine nature.

Fill these waters, we pray, with the power of that same
    Spirit
that all who enter them may be reborn, rise from the
    grave to new life,
and be conformed to the image of Christ.

As the apostles and prophets, the confessors and martyrs
faithfully served you in their generation
may we be built into an eternal dwelling for you
through Jesus Christ, our Lord,
to whom with you and the Holy Spirit
be honour and glory, now and for ever.[22]

Notes

1 Conversation with History

1 Michael Ignatieff, *The Russian Album* (London: Penguin, 1987), p. [5].
2 See W. H. Frere ed., *Visitation Articles and Injunctions of the Period of the Reformation*, Vol. III, Alcuin Club Collections 16 (London: Longmans, 1910), p. 69, The 'Interpretations of the Bishops', 1560–1; p. 109, The Royal Order, 1561; p. 176, Archbishop Parker's Advertisements, 1566; and pp. 199 and 377, Archbishop Parker's Articles for the Norwich and Winchester Dioceses.
3 Mike Salter, *The Old Parish Churches of Shropshire* (Malvern: Folly Publications, 1992).
4 I am indebted to Prebendary Ralph Garnett for supplying this information.

2 Setting the Scene

1 See *Modern Eucharistic Agreement* (London: SPCK, 1973), pp. 1–31. See also pp. vf., for Foreword by Bishop Clark.
2 See Bryan Spinks, 'Luther's Timely Theology of Unilateral Baptism', *Lutheran Quarterly* 9 (1995), pp. 23–45, and 'Calvin's Baptismal Theology and the Making of the Strasbourg and Genevan Baptismal Liturgies 1540 and 1552', *Scottish Journal of Theology* 48 (1995), pp. 55–78.
3 See, for example, Kenneth Stevenson, 'Patterns of Christian Initiation' in David R. Holeton, ed., *Growing in Newness of Life: Christian Initiation in Anglicanism Today* (Toronto: Anglican Book Centre, 1993), pp. 137–49.
4 See B. A. Gerrish, *Grace and Gratitude: The Eucharistic Theol-*

ogy of John Calvin (Edinburgh: T & T Clark, 1993), p. 167; Gerrish, 'The Lord's Supper in the Reformed Confessions', in Donald K. McKin, ed., *Major Themes in the Reformed Tradition* (Grand Rapids: Eerdmans, 1992), pp. 245–58; see also Bryan Spinks, 'Karl Barth's Teaching on Baptism: Its Development, Antecedents and the "Liturgical Factor" ', *Ecclesia Orans* 14 (1997), pp. 261–88.

5 Text in F. E. Brightman, *The English Rite*, vol. II (London: Rivingtons, 1915), pp. 728 ff. See also Jean Deshusses, *Les Sacramentaire Grégorien: ses principales formes d'après les plus anciens manuscrits romains* I, Spicilegium Friburgense 16 (Fribourg: éditions universitaires, 1971), no. 1074, pp. 374 ff. For Luther's 1523 and Osiander's Baptismal Rites, see J. D. C. Fisher, *Christian Initiation: The Reformation Period: Some early Reformed rites of Baptism and Confirmation and other Contemporary Documents*, Alcuin Club Collections 51 (London: SPCK, 1970), pp. 9 and 19. See Augustine, *Sermo* 132.1; see also William Harmless, *Augustine and the Catechumenate*, a Pueblo Book (Collegeville: The Liturgical Press, 1995), p. 172.

6 Gordon Jeanes, 'A Reformation Treatise on the Sacraments', *Journal of Theological Studies* 46.1 (1995), pp. 161 ff. and pp. 170 ff. See also Brightman, *English Rite*, pp. 730 ff. Luther's second 'Taufbüchlein' was completed in 1526.

7 See *The Works of John Jewell* III, Parker Society (Cambridge: Cambridge University Press, 1848), pp. 460–5, for Jewel's original statement on baptism, followed by Harding's answer, followed by Jewel's reply.

8 Augustine, *Epp.* 23; see Jewel, *Works*, p. 463. (This was a theological commonplace among the Early Fathers.)

9 See Brightman, *English Rite*, pp. 741 ff. The signing with the cross was placed after baptism in 1552, to strengthen the motif of discipleship; in 1549, it had been *before* the baptism, as in the medieval rites. Martin Bucer's *Censura* of the 1549 Prayer Book allowed its use, as long as it was properly understood; see E. C. Whitaker, ed., *Martin Bucer and the Book of Common Prayer*, Alcuin Club Collections 53 (Great Wakering: Mayhew-McCrimmon, 1974), p. 90.

10 See Edward Cardwell, *A History of Conferences and Other Proceedings connected with the Revision of the Book of*

Common Prayer from the year 1558 to the year 1690 (Oxford: Oxford University Press, 1840), p. 40. See also pp. 138 ff. on the Hampton Court Conference 1604.

11 See W. H. Frere and C. E. Douglas, eds., *Puritan Manifestoes: A Study of the Origin of the Puritan Revolt*, Church Historical Society (London: SPCK, 1907), pp. 26 ff. and 117.

12 See John Ayre, ed., *The Works of John Whitgift*, Parker Society (Cambridge: Cambridge University Press, 1851–3), vols. I, pp. 99, 130, 216, 207–12; II, pp. 456–8, 461–4, 495–540; III, pp. 14–17, 22–4, 86–7, 109–49, 381–3, 492–3, 546–7, 553. (Cartwright's contentions are printed in full next to Whitgift's answers.) See also *A Replie to an Answere made by M. Doctor Whitgift against the Admonition to the Parliament* (1573), pp. 142, 139–47, 169, 170–2; and *The Rest of the Second Replie* (1577), pp. 116–43, 216–34. See also John F. H. New, 'The Whitgift–Cartwright Controversy', *Archiv für Reformationsgeschichte* 59 (1968), pp. 203–11. The cross received special defence in the 1604 Canons on the grounds of the preaching of the cross as central to the Christian religion, the reverence with which the cross was received by early Christians at baptism, and the need to keep a useful ceremony, rather than abolish it, simply because Roman Catholics abused it. See *The Constitutions and Canons Ecclesiastical and Thirty-Nine Articles of the Church of England* (London: SPCK, 1843), pp. 16–19.

13 Gordon Donaldson, *The Making of the Scottish Prayer Book of 1637* (Edinburgh: Edinburgh University Press, 1954), pp. 24–6.

14 See *The Folger Library Edition of the Works of Richard Hooker* vol. 6, part 2, Medieval and Renaissance Texts and Studies (New York: Binghampton, 1993), p. 764.

3 *Inward or Outward?* William Perkins (1558–1602)

1 See for example Edward Yarnold, SJ, *The Awe Inspiring Rites of Initiation: Baptismal Homilies in the Fourth Century* (Slough: St Paul Publications, 1971); and Enrico Mazza, *Mystagogy* (New York: Pueblo, 1989). See also, to counterbalance any uniform picture, Paul Bradshaw, *The Search for the Origins of Christian Worship* (London: SPCK, 1992), pp. 161–84.

2 J. D. C. Fisher *Christian Initiation: Baptism in the Medieval West – A Study in the Disintegration of the Primitive Rite of Initiation*, Alcuin Club Collections 47 (London: SPCK, 1965).

3 See Walter Hilton, *The Scale of Perfection*, newly edited with introduction by Evelyn Underhill (London: Watkins, 1948), especially book 2, chapter 6, pp. 243 ff. See also John Clark, 'Confession and Re-formation: Walter Hilton's Sacramental Theology' in David Brown and Ann Loades, eds., *Christ: The Sacramental Word: Incarnation, Sacrament and Poetry.* (London: SPCK, 1996), pp. 143–53. See also Adrian Hastings, 'Walter Hilton', The Eighth Southwell Lecture (Thursday, October 17th, 1996).

4 J. I. Packer, 'An Anglican to Remember: William Perkins: Puritan Populariser' (St Antholin's Lectureship Charity Lecture 1996); Ian Breward, ed., *The Work of William Perkins*, Courtenay Library of Reformation Classics 3 (Abingdon: The Sutton Courtenay Press, 1970). This latter also contains a detailed introduction, pp. 3–131. (Hereafter referred to as Breward.)

5 See Breward, pp. 175–259. See also *The Works of that Famous and Worthy Minister of Christ in the University of Cambridge, Mr. William Perkins*, vol. I (London: John Leggatt, 1626). The table referred to, which Breward does not reproduce, is to be found between pp. 72 and 73.

6 Breward, p. 177.

7 Ibid., pp. 213–24.

8 Ibid., p. 213.

9 See Kenneth Stevenson, *Covenant of Grace Renewed: A Vision of the Eucharist in the 17th Century* (London: Darton, Longman & Todd, 1994), pp. 51 and 65 n.13.

10 See Breward, p. 214.

11 Ibid., p. 217.

12 Ibid., p. 221.

13 Ibid., p. 222.

14 Ibid., p. 219.

15 Ibid., p. 220.

16 *The Works of that Famous and Worthy Minister of Christ in the University of Cambridge, Mr. William Perkins II* (London: John Legatt, 1631), pp. 255–64. (Hereafter referred to as *Galatians*).

17 Ibid., p. 256.
18 Ibid., p. 257.
19 Ibid., p. 258.
20 Ibid., p. 260.
21 Ibid., p. 261.
22 Ibid., p. 262.
23 Ibid., p. 263.
24 Ibid., p. 265.
25 Ibid., p. 266.
26 See *The Works of that Famous and Worthy Minister of Christ in the University of Cambridge, Mr. William Perkins*, vol. II, pp. 572–4.
27 Breward, pp. 331–49.
28 Ibid., p. 345.

4 *Sharing in the Life of God:* Richard Hooker (1554–1600)

1 John Booty in the *Folger Library Edition of the Works of Richard Hooker*, vol. 6 part 1, pp. 197 ff. (Hereafter referred to as *Works*). See also A. M. Allchin, *Participation in God: a Forgotten Strand in Anglican Tradition* (London: Darton, Longman & Todd, 1988), and Rowan Williams' article, 'Deification' in Gordon S. Wakefield, ed., *A Dictionary of Christian Spirituality* (London: SCM Press, 1983), pp. 106–8.
2 See Richard Bauckham, 'Hooker, Travers and The Church of Rome in the 1580's', *Journal of Ecclesiastical History* 29 (1978), pp. 37–50.
3 *Laws of Ecclesiastical Polity* II 11.2. *The Works of that Learned and Judicious Divine Mr Richard Hooker* (arranged by John Keble, revised by R. W. Church and F. Paget) II (Oxford: Clarendon Press, 1887).
4 *Works*, pp. 183 ff.
5 See Stevenson, *Covenant of Grace Renewed*, pp. 23 ff. and for discussion of Hooker, particularly in relation to the Eucharist, pp. 19–38.
6 *Laws* V 56.1.
7 Ibid., V 77.8.
8 See also, exceptionally, Frances Paget, *An Introduction to the Fifth Book of Hooker's Treatise of Laws of Ecclesiastical Polity*

(Oxford: Clarendon Press, 1907) pp. 206–16, for a brief discussion of his treatment of baptism. See also the commentary in the Folger Edition, *Works*, pp. 729–64.

9 See *Works*, pp. 187 ff. and table on p. 189.

10 *Laws* V 58.1.

11 Ibid., V 58.4.

12 Ibid., V 59.5.

13 Ibid., V 60.1.

14 Ibid., V 60.2.

15 See Stevenson, *Covenant of Grace Renewed*, p. 27, and p. 37 nn. 19 & 20. See in particular, Edward Yarnold. '*Duplex Iustitia*; the 16th century and the 20th', in G. R. Evans, ed., *Christian Authority: Essays in honour of Henry Chadwick* (Oxford: Clarendon Press, 1988), pp. 204–23.

16 *Laws* V 60.6.

17 Ibid., 60.7.

18 Ibid., V 61.4.

19 Ibid., V 62.5.

20 Ibid., V 62.12.

21 Ibid., V 62.15.

22 Ibid., V 62.19.

23 Ibid., V 63.1.

24 Ibid., V 63.3; Isidore of Seville, *De officiis ecclesiasticis* 2.24.

25 *Laws* V 64.1.

26 Ibid., V 64.4. For 'superstitious toyes' and 'toying foolishly', see *Puritan Manifestoes*, p. 26 (*First Admonition*); and 'trifling and toying', see *The Works of William Whitgift* III, p. 115 (Cartwright's *Defence of the Admonition*).

27 See Brightman, *The English Rite*, pp. 728 and 741.

28 *Laws* V 65.2.

29 Ibid., V 625.4.

30 See St Augustine, *Confessions*, translated with an Introduction by Henry Chadwick (Oxford: Clarendon Press, 1991), book X, for a modern English translation. See also Kenneth Stevenson, *Handing On: Borderlands of Worship and Tradition* (London: Darton, Longman & Todd 1996), pp. 24 ff.

31 *Laws* V 65.6, 8, 9, 10, 11, 16.

32 Ibid., V 65.21.

33 Ibid., V 66.1.

34 Ibid., V 66.6.

35 See Paget's Introduction, pp. 317ff: to which I can add my own edition printed by Richard Bishop in 1639.

36 The references to Cartwright are to be found in *Laws* V 59.1, 60.1, 60.3, 60.5, 60.7, 61.1, 61.3, 61.4, 62.1, 62.13, 62.14, 62.18, 62.19, 62.20, 62.22, 64.1, 64.3, 64.5, 65.3, 65.4, 65.6, 65.12, and 66.8.

37 Olivier Loyer, *L'anglicanisme de Richard Hooker: Thèse présentée devant l'université de Paris III – le 1 juin 1977* (Paris: Librairie Honoré Champion, 1979) Tome 1, p. 506.

5 *Heaven Opened:* Lancelot Andrewes (1555–1600)

1 Stevenson, *Handling On*, pp. 131 ff. See also p. 142 n. 15; John Sweet, *Revelation* (London: SCM Press, 1990), p. 115.

2 See Chapter 2, pp. 13–4 and n. 5.

3 *Ninety-Six Sermons by Lancelot Andrewes*, Vol. 3, Library of Anglo-Catholic Theology (Oxford: Parker, 1841), pp. 241–60 (Sermon Series hereafter referred to as *Sermons* with volume number). See also Stevenson, *Covenant of Grace Renewed*, pp. 39–66; Stevenson, *Handing On*, pp. 66–82, and Stevenson, '"Human Nature Honoured". Absolution in Lancelot Andrewes', in Martin Dudley, ed., *Like a Two-Edged Sword – The Word of God in Liturgy and History; Essays in honour of Canon Donald Gray* (Norwich: Canterbury Press, 1995), pp. 113–38. See also Nicholas Lossky, *Lancelot Andrewes The Preacher (1555–1626): The Origins of the Mystical Theology of the Church of England* (Oxford: Clarendon Press, 1991). For the life of Andrewes, see R. L. Ottley, *Lancelot Andrewes* (London: Methuen, 1894); and Paul Welsby, *Lancelot Andrewes 1555–1626* (London: SPCK, 1958). See also A. M. Allchin, 'Lancelot Andrewes', in Geoffrey Rowell, ed., *The English Religious Tradition and the Genius of Anglicanism* (Wantage: Ikon Books, 1992), pp. 145–64.

4 See Lossky, *Lancelot Andrewes The Preacher*, pp. 208–88.

5 See Stevenson, *Handing On*, pp. 78–81, for discussion of this sermon.

6 *Sermons* III p. 241.

7 Ibid., III p. 242.

8 Ibid., III p. 199. See also the 1600 Sermon on Absolution, *Sermons* V pp. 89 ff.; and also above, n. 3, Stevenson, ' "Human Nature Honoured" ', pp. 116 ff.

9 *Sermons* III p. 242.

10 See Whitsun Sermon 4 (1611) in Ibid., III, p. 169.

11 Ibid., III p. 243.

12 Ibid., III p. 244.

13 Ibid., III pp. 244–5.

14 Ibid., III p. 246. Ambrose, for example, commenting on this very text, takes this view, see *In Lk* 3:21.

15 See Chapter 3 pp. 30f. In the Easter Sermon 14 (1620), Andrewes refers to the old name of the first Sunday after Easter as 'In albis', harking back to the custom of the newly baptized wearing white on that occasion. See *Sermons* III, p. 9.

16 *Sermons* III p. 247. For the streams of water and blood, see the sacramental imagery used in Sermon on Good Friday I (1597), *Sermons* II p. 139. See also Cardwell, *A History of Conferences*, pp. 197 ff.

17 *Sermons* III p. 248.

18 Ibid., III p. 249; compare Hooker, *Laws* V, 59.5.

19 *Sermons* III p. 250.

20 Ibid., III p. 251.

21 Ibid., III p. 252.

22 See Welsby, *Lancelot Andrewes,* pp. 135 ff.

23 *Sermons* III pp. 254–5.

24 Ibid., III p. 256.

25 *Tract. in Jn* 80:3. The Latin original is 'accedit verbum', indicative, whereas Andrewes has made it a jussive subjunctive. (No actual citation is given by Andrewes.)

26 *Sermons* III p. 257.

27 Ibid., III p. 258.

28 Ibid., III p. 259.

29 Lossky, *Lancelot Andrewes The Preacher*, p. 349.

30 Sermon on Prayer 7, see *Sermons* V p. 367.

31 See *The Preces Privatae of Lancelot Andrewes Bishop of Winchester*, translated with an introduction and notes by F. E. Brightman (London: Methuen, 1903), p. 212.

32 See Lossky, *Lancelot Andrewes The Preacher*, p. 274.

33 Kenneth Fincham, ed., *Visitation Articles and Injunctions of the*

Early Stuart Church, vol. I, Church of England Record Society (Bury St Edmunds: Boydel Press, 1995).

34 *Sermons* IV pp. 84–5 (Gowries 4 Sermon, 1613); and *Sermons* III p. 169 (Whitsun 4 Sermon, 1611), a discussion of Ephesians 4:30, interestingly the only sermon preached on the festival before the Royal Court at Windsor.

35 Lossky, *Lancelot Andrewes The Preacher*, p. 349.

36 Since the completion of this work, Marianne Dorman has shown me her transcription of some unpublished catechetical lectures delivered by Andrewes to the boys of Westminster School, and acquired by Lambeth Palace Library in 1994; these throw fresh light on Andrewes' view of original sin (noticeably not mentioned at all in the 1615 Whitsun Sermon) as anticipating some of Taylor's views (see below, Chapter 8). It is to be hoped that Dr Dorman's work on Lambeth Palace ms. 3707 will see the light of day.

6 *Providence:* George Herbert (1593–1633)

1 Hooker, *Laws* V 60.7. See Chapter 4 p. 46, n.17.

2 See Chapter 3.

3 See Stevenson, *Handing On*, pp. 17–32, and nn., pp. 134–5.

4 St Augustine, *Confessions* IX.vi(14), p. 164.

5 See Harmless, *Augustine and the Catechumenate*, pp. 39 ff.

6 *Confessions* I.i(1), p. 3.

7 See Stephen Sykes, *Unashamed Anglicanism* (London: Darton, Longman & Todd, 1995), pp. 3–23, for a discussion of some of these issues in the chapter entitled 'Baptisme doth represente unto us oure Profession'.

8 Stanley Stewart, *George Herbert*, Twayne's English Authors' Series (Boston: Twayne Publishers, 1986), pp. 1–24. See also J. R. Watson, 'George Herbert and the English Hymn', *Theology* 794 (March–April 1997), pp. 101–8.

9 *Izaak Walton's Life of George Herbert*, With a preface by Canon Patrick Magee (Salisbury: Perdix Press, 1988).

10 T. S. Eliot, *George Herbert*, with an introduction by Peter Porter, Writers and their work (Plymouth: Northcote House Publishers, 1994), p. 20.

11 Nigel Yates, *Buildings, Faith and Worship: The Liturgical*

Arrangements of Anglican Churches 1600–1900 (Oxford: Clarendon Press, 1991), pp. 33, 115, and see plate 16a.

12 Stewart, *George Herbert*, p. 41.

13 *The English Poems of George Herbert with a Priest to the Temple and his Collection of Proverbs called 'Jacula Prudentium'*, The Ancient & Modern Library of Theological Literature (London: Griffith, Farran Oakden & Welsh, n. d.), pp. 212 ff.

14 Brightman, *English Rite* II, pp. 732–5. The prayer is adapted from Hermann Von Wied's 'Didagma' (1543).

15 See for example Stewart, *George Herbert*, pp. 25 ff.

16 See *The Works of George Herbert*, edited with commentary by F. E. Hutchinson (Oxford: Clarendon Press, 1941), pp. 43 ff.

17 Ibid., pp. 6, 25.

18 Ibid., pp. 56, 102. See also Elizabeth Clarke, 'George Herbert's *The Temple*: The Genius of Anglicanism and the Inspiration for Poetry', in Geoffrey Rowell, ed., *The English Tradition and The Genius of Anglicanism*, p. [140].

19 See *The Works of George Herbert*, pp. 43–4.

20 Ibid., p. 44.

21 See *Select Hymns taken out of Mr Herbert's Temple and turned into the Common Metre: to be Sung in the Tunes Ordinarily Used in Church* (London: Bridge, 1697).

22 See *The Poems of George Herbert*, with an Introduction by Arthur Waugh (Oxford: Oxford University Press, 1907), p. 222.

23 Stewart, *George Herbert*, p. 30.

24 For Latin text, see *The Poems of George Herbert*, p. 231. I am indebted to Colin Bradley for supplying this translation.

25 For Latin text, see *The Poems of George Herbert*, pp. 231 ff. I am indebted to Colin Bradley for supplying this translation.

26 See *The English Poems of George Herbert*, p. 187.

7 *What About the Unbaptized?* John Bramhall (1594–1663)

1 See Fisher, *Christian Initiation*, pp. 101 ff.

2 William Langland, *The Vision of Piers Plowman*, a complete edition of the B-text, edited by A. V. C. Schmidt, Everyman's Library (London: Dent, 1987), Passus XI, lines 80, 81, 83, p. 120.

3 See above, Chapter 4.

4 See *The Works of John Bramhall*, Library of Anglo-Catholic Theology (Oxford: Parker, 1842), vol. I, pp. iii–xi, for a life of Bramhall. For 'a short discourse on persons dying without baptism' (hereafter 'Discourse'), see pp. 171–80.

5 On Bramhall see F. R. Bolton, *The Caroline Tradition of the Church of Ireland with Particular Reference to Bishop Jeremy Taylor*, Church Historical Society (London: SPCK, 1958), pp. 8 ff. and *passim*.

6 As Bolton notes, 'if as bishop of Derry he had promoted the influence of the Church of England, as Primate he sought to preserve the freedom of the national church', *ibid.*, p. 35.

7 See *The Works of John Bramhall* I, p. xxxiv.

8 Robert S. Bosher, *The Making of the Restoration Settlement: The Influence of the Laudians 1649–1662* (London: Dacre Press, 1951), p. 58.

9 'Discourse', p. 171.

10 See T. S. Eliot, *For Lancelot Andrewes: Essays on Style and Order* (London: Faber, 1970), p. 32.

11 'Discourse', p. 172.

12 Ibid.

13 See above, Chapter 3.

14 'Discourse', pp. 172–3.

15 Ibid., pp. 173–8.

16 See Bolton, *The Caroline Tradition*, pp. 76 ff.

17 'Discourse', pp. 178–80.

18 See Bolton, *The Caroline Tradition*, p. 121. A large part of this is to be found among the Hastings papers in the Henry Huntington Library at San Marino, California.

19 Bolton, *The Caroline Tradition*, p. 124.

20 See H. R. McAdoo, *The Spirit of Anglicanism: A Survey of Anglican Theological Method in the 17th Century* (London: A & C Black, 1965), p. 372 (quotation) and pp. 368–85 for discussion of his work.

21 See Eliot, *For Lancelot Andrewes*, pp. 31 ff. and McAdoo, *Spirit of Anglicanism*, pp. 379 ff.

8 *Holy Living:* Jeremy Taylor (1613–67)

1 See Owen Chadwick, *Michael Ramsey, A Life* (Oxford: Clarendon Press, 1990).

2 Robert F. Taft, ' "Holy Things for the Saints": The Ancient Call to Communion and its response', in Gerard Austin, ed., *Fountain of Life: in Memory of Niels K Rasmussen, O.P.* (Washington: The Pastoral Press, 1991), pp. 87–102.

3 A. M. Allchin, 'Holiness in the Anglican Tradition', in Marina Chavchavadze, ed., *Man's Concern with Holiness* (London: Hodder and Stoughton, 1970), p. 37 (whole essay, pp. 37–58).

4 See Hugh Ross Williamson, *Jeremy Taylor* (London: Dobson, 1952) and C. J. Stranks, *The Life and Writings of Jeremy Taylor*, Church Historical Society (London: SPCK, 1952).

5 See Stevenson, *Covenant of Grace Renewed*, pp. 110–26, and nn., pp. 133–4.

6 *The Rule and Exercises of Holy Living*, chapter 4, additional section 6, 'A Prayer to be said on our Birthday or Day of Baptism'. Taylor is not unique in making provision for a prayer on such an occasion: cf. a similar prayer, albeit with different imagery, in *John Cosin: A Collection of Private Devotions*, ed. Peter Stanwood and Daniel O'Connor (Oxford: Clarendon Press, 1967), pp. 292 f. John Cosin's prayers were published in 1627.

7 See *The Whole Works of the Rt Revd Jeremy Taylor*, ed. Reginald Heber [Vols. II and III,] (London: Rivingtons, 1828). See also Henry McAdoo, *First of Its Kind; Jeremy Taylor's Life of Christ, A Study in the Functioning of a Moral Theology* (Norwich: Canterbury Press, 1994).

8 *The Great Exemplar*, Part III Section XVI, and Part I Section IX. For which compare Chapter 5, p. 62f.

9 Harry Boone Porter, *Jeremy Taylor Liturgist*, Alcuin Club Collection 61 (London: SPCK, 1979), p. 30.

10 *Great Exemplar* Part I, Discourse VI.I.

11 See Chapter 10, p. 131ff.

12 *Great Exemplar*, Discourse VI.I. 11.

13 Ibid., Discourse VI.I. 14–28.

14 Ibid., Discourse VI.II. 1–11.

15 Ibid., Discourse VI.II. 12–24.

16 Ibid., Discourse VI.II. 25–34.

17 Ian Breward, ed., *The Westminster Directory*, Grove Liturgical Study 21 (Bramcote: Grove Books 1980), pp. 19–21.

18 Porter, *Jeremy Taylor Liturgist*, between pp. 40–1. See also the important discussion by Bryan Spinks, 'Two Seventeenth Century Examples of "Lex credendi Lex orandi": The Baptismal and Eucharistic Theologies and Liturgies of Jeremy Taylor and Richard Baxter', *Studia Liturgica* 21.2 (1991), pp. 165–89.

19 See Porter, *Jeremy Taylor Liturgist*, pp. 33 ff. See also 'A Discourse of Confirmation', in *The Whole Works of The Rt Revd Jeremy Taylor*, vol. XI.II, pp. ccix–ccxxvii (Epistle Dedicatory), and pp. 229–97. See also S. L. Ollard, 'Confirmation in the Anglican Communion', in *Confirmation or The Laying On Of Hands*, vol. I (London: SPCK, 1926), pp. 154–62.

20 See Chapter 4, pp. 50f.

21 McAdoo, *First of Its Kind*, pp. 9 ff.

9 *Disciples of Christ:* Richard Baxter (1615–91)

1 See Chapter 3, p. 26ff.

2 See Chapter 8, p. 103.

3 See Geoffrey Nuttall, *Richard Baxter* (London: Nelson, 1965); J. I. Packer, 'A Man for All Ministries; Richard Baxter 1615–1691', (St Antholin's Lectureship, Charity Lecture, 1991); and also the Introduction by James Packer in Richard Baxter, *The Reformed Pastor*, edited by William Brown (Edinburgh: Banner of Truth Trust, 1979), pp. 9–19.

4 Packer, 'A Man for All Ministries', p. 16.

5 *The Poetical Fragments of Richard Baxter* (London: Pickering, 1821), pp. 147, 149.

6 From the poem entitled 'The Return', in *Poetical Fragments*, p. 87.

7 See 'Confirmation and Restoration. The Necessary Means of Reformation and Reconciliation' in *The Works of Richard Baxter*, edited by W. Orme, vol. XIV (London: Duncan, 1838), pp. 415 ff.

8 See Spinks, 'Two Seventeenth Century Examples', *Studia Liturgica* 21.2 (1991), pp. 165–89.

9 Quoted in Nuttall, *Richard Baxter*, p. 55 and also in Spinks, 'Two Seventeenth Century Examples', pp. 172 ff.

10 Spinks, 'Two Seventeenth Century Examples', p. 173.

11 See Chapter 8, pp. 106f.

12 For an account of this conference and the surrounding events, see G. J. Cuming, *A History of Anglican Liturgy* (London: Macmillan, 1982, 2nd edition), pp. 116 ff.

13 See *A Petition for Peace: With the Reformation of the Liturgy as it was presented to the Right Reverend Bishops by the Divines appointed by His Majesties Commission* (London: 1661), pp. 58 ff.

14 See 'Confirmation and Restoration', pp. 401–594. For the text in the 'Savoy Liturgy', see *A Petition for Peace*, pp. 65 and following. See also S. L. Ollard, 'Confirmation in the Anglican Communion', in *Confirmation or the Laying On of Hands*, pp. 140–3.

15 See 'The Catechizing of Families' in *The Practical Works of The Reverend Richard Baxter*, edited by W. Orme, vol. XIX (London: Duncan, 1830), pp. 261–74.

16 See Chapter 3, pp. 25ff.

17 See Chapter 4, p. 47.

18 Horton Davies, *Worship and Theology in England: From Andrewes to Baxter and Fox 1603–1690* (Princeton: Princeton University Press, 1975), p. 524.

19 See Spinks, 'Two Seventeenth Century Examples'.

20 See Stevenson, *Covenant of Grace Renewed*, pp. 110–35.

10 *Professing the Faith:* Simon Patrick (1626–1707)

1 For the real history see J. N. D. Kelly, *Early Christian Creeds* (London: Longmans, 1950), especially pp. 1–52.

2 See Chapter 3, p. 27ff.

3 See Chapter 4, p. 47f.

4 See Chapter 9, pp. 116ff.

5 See Chapter 8, p. 108.

6 See *Initiation Services: A Report by the Liturgical Commission*, GS1152 (London: Church House, 1995), pp. 22 & 47.

7 See Chapter 6, pp. 72ff.

8 See Stevenson, *Covenant of Grace Renewed*, pp. 149–63; Stevenson, 'The eucharistic theology of Simon Patrick' in Carsten Bach-Nielsen, Susanne Gregersen and Ninna Jørgensen,

eds., *Ordet, Kirken og Kulturen: Afhandlinger om Kristendolms Historie tilegnet Jakob Balling* (Åarhus: Universitets Forlag, 1993), pp. 363–78; Stevenson, 'The *Mensa Mystica* of Simon Patrick (1626–1707): A Case-Study in Restoration Eucharistic Piety', in Nathan Mitchell, John F. Baldovin SJ, eds., *Rule of Prayer, Rule of Faith: Essays in Honor of Aidan Kavanagh O.S.B.*, a Pueblo Book (Collegeville: The Liturgical Press, 1996), pp. 161–99. See also McAdoo, *Spirit of Anglicanism* pp. 189–97.

9 John Spurr, *The Restoration Church of England 1646–1689* (New Haven and London: Yale University Press, 1991), p. 348.

10 See *The Works of Simon Patrick DD Including his Autobiography*, edited by Alexander Taylor (Oxford: Oxford University Press, 1858), vol. I, pp. 65 ff., and vol. II, pp. 1–92. See also the works cited in note 8 above.

11 See *Works of Simon Patrick*, I, pp. 1-64 (*Aqua Genitalis*).

12 See McAdoo, *Spirit of Anglicanism*, pp. 81–155.

13 *Works of Simon Patrick*, IV, p. 506.

14 Ibid., IV, p. 652.

15 Ibid., IV, pp. 1–396.

16 *Aqua Genitalis*, pp. 3, 5.

17 Ibid., pp. 11–38.

18 Ibid., pp. 39–59.

19 See Chapter 3, pp. 24ff.

20 See Kenneth Stevenson, *Nuptial Blessing: A Study of Christian Marriage Rites*, Alcuin Club Collections 64 (London: SPCK, 1982), pp. 138 ff.

21 *Works of Simon Patrick*, vol. IX, pp. 332 ff.

22 *Aqua Genitalis*, p. 25.

23 McAdoo, *Spirit of Anglicanism*, p. 190.

11 *'Covenant Begun and Continued'*: Herbert Thorndike (1598–1672)

1 See, for example, R. E. Clements, *Prophecy and Covenant*, Studies in Biblical Theology 43 (London: SCM Press, 1965).

2 See E. C. Miller, jr., 'The Doctrine of the Church in the Thought of Herbert Thorndike (1598–1672)', Oxford University D.Phil.

Dissertation 1990, p. 139. It is to be hoped that this excellent study will one day be published.

3 See David H. Tripp, *The Renewal of the Covenant in the Methodist Tradition* (London: Epworth, 1969), especially pp. 116–18, 123–4, 140–1, 148, 149, 159–61, 184–5, 212.

4 *The Methodist Service Book* (London: Methodist Publishing House, 1975), p. D.10.

5 See T. A. Lacey, *Herbert Thorndike, 1598–1672* (London: SPCK, 1929).

6 See Peter Levi, *Eden Renewed: the Public and Private Life of John Milton* (London: Macmillan, 1996), p. 18.

7 See 'Of the Government of Churches: A Discourse pointing at the Primitive Form', in *The Theological Works of Herbert Thorndike*, vol. I, Library of Anglo-Catholic Theology (Oxford: Parker, 1844) pp. 1–97.

8 See Chapter 10, p. 129.

9 See Jocelyn Perkins, *Westminster Abbey, Its Worship and Ornaments*, vol. III, Alcuin Club Collections 38 (London: Oxford University Press, 1952), p. 41. I am indebted to Dr Richard Mortimer, Keeper of the Muniments, Westminster Abbey, for information about this.

10 Lacey, *Herbert Thorndike*, pp. 29, 67.

11 See Westminster Abbey Library, Th MS 3/013 and 3/045 (incomplete).

12 See Chapter 4 on Andrewes and Chapter 8 on Taylor, pp. 58ff, 100ff.

13 See Westminster Abbey Library, Th MS 3/031, 3/032, 3/033, 3/034, 3/035, 3/036.

14 See Westminster Abbey Library, Th MS 3/031, pp. 4–5.

15 See Westminster Abbey Library, Th MS 2/1/4, pp. 1, 4, 6.

16 *The Theological Works of Herbert Thorndike*, vols II, III, & IV.

17 Bosher, *Making of the Restoration Settlement*, p. 93.

18 *Works of Herbert Thorndike* III, pp. 2–15.

19 Ibid., III, p. 13.

20 Ibid., III, pp. 15–29.

21 See Brightman, *English Rite* II, p. 765.

22 *Works of Herbert Thorndike* III, pp. 29–40.

23 Ibid., III, pp. 40–54.

24 Ibid., III, p. 47 n. h.
25 The answers given at baptism must be based on 'Man's free choice'.
26 *Works of Herbert Thorndike* III, p. 64 n. f.
27 In the third part of the *Epilogue* entitled *The Laws of The Church*, Thorndike returns to some of these themes. See *Works* IV, pp. 733–52.
28 Paul Avis, *Anglicanism and The Christian Church: Theological Resources in Historical Perspective* (Edinburgh: T & T Clark, 1989), p. 150.
29 Westminster Abbey ThMS 3/045 p. 1. I am deeply indebted to Dr Charles Miller for his assistance with Thorndike.

12 Retrospect

1 F. D. Maurice, *The Kingdom of Christ*, vol. I (London: Rivingtons, 1842), pp. xxviii and xxix. See also Alec Vidler, *The Theology of F. D. Maurice* (London: SCM Press, 1948), pp. 94–120.
2 Augustine, *Confessions* X.x. (15), p. 187.
3 *Laws* V 67. 1.
4 *Galatians*, p. 265: see Chapter 3, pp. 33.
5 See Chapter 3, pp. 22ff, table and n. 12.
6 Breward p. 217: see Chapter 3, p. 26.
7 *Laws* V 56. 1.
8 Ibid., V 62.12.
9 *Sermons* III p. 242.
10 Ibid., III p. 247.
11 *The Works of George Herbert*, p. 43–4.
12 'Discourse', pp. 171–80.
13 *Holy Living*, chapter 4, additional section 6.
14 *Great Exemplar*, Discourse VI. I. 28.
15 Ibid., Discourse XI. II. 8.
16 'The Catechizing of Families', pp. 261–74.
17 *Aqua Genitalis*, p. 30.
18 *Works of Herbert Thorndike*, pp. 12–15.
19 Brightman, *English Rite* II, pp. 7, 27 ff.
20 See Chapter 2, pp. 13f and n. 5.
21 See *The Constitutions and Canons Ecclesiastical*, pp. 16–19.

22 See Robert S. Paul, *The Assembly of the Lord: Politics and Religion in the Westminster Assembly and the 'Grand Debate'* (Edinburgh: T & T Clark, 1985), pp. 373–5, 392–3, 412 n. 106, 439 n. 10.

23 See above, n. 20.

24 Alan Torrance, *Persons in Communion: Trinitarian Description and Human Participation* (Edinburgh: T & T Clark, 1996), pp. 59 f.; quotation p. 60.

25 *Great Exemplar*, Discourse XII.18.

26 See Chapter 8, p. 108.

27 See Chapter 2, pp. 12f and n. 4.

28 Brightman, *English Rite* II, p. 732; 1662 'Congregation' was changed to 'Church', in line with other alterations elsewhere in the Prayer Book.

29 *The Thirty-Nine Articles of The Church of England explained with an Introduction by Edgar Gibson*, vol. II (London: Methuen, 1897), p. 620.

30 *Aqua Genitalis*, p. 25.

13 Prospect

1 Whitsun Sermon 14, *Sermons* III pp. 362.

2 See Kenneth Stevenson and David Stancliffe, 'Christian Initiation and Its Relation to Some Pastoral Offices', *Theology* 760 (July/August 1991), pp. 284–91.

3 See, for example, *The Book of Common Prayer* (New York: Church Hymnal Corporation and Seabury Press, 1979), pp. 299–314: see also the essays in David R. Holeton, ed., *Growing in Newness of Life: Christian Initiation in Anglicanism Today*. See also Aidan Kavanagh, *The Shape of Baptism* (New York: Pueblo, 1974).

4 Pierre-Marie Gy, 'The Idea of "Christian Initiation"', *Studia Liturgica* 12 (1977), pp. 172–5. An expanded version of this paper appears as 'La notion chrétienne d'initiation', *La Maison-Dieu* 132 (1977), pp. 33–54. (Republished in Pierre-Marie Gy, *La liturgie dans l' histoire* (Paris: Cerf, 1990), pp. 17–39.)

5 *Capitula Coelestini* 8. See also Alexander Schmemann, *Introduction to Liturgical Theology* (New York: St Vladimir's Press,

1975); Geoffrey Wainwright, *Doxology: The Praise of God in Worship, Doctrine and Life* (London: Epworth, 1980); Aidan Kavanagh, *On Liturgical Theology* (New York: Pueblo, 1984). See also Maxwell Johnson, 'Liturgy and Theology', in Paul Bradshaw and Bryan Spinks, eds., *Liturgy in Dialogue: Essays in Memory of Ronald Jasper* (London: SPCK, 1993), pp. 202–25.

6 See Stevenson, *Covenant of Grace Renewed*, p. 185; see also Kenneth Stevenson, *Eucharist and Offering*, with foreword by Mark Santer (New York: Pueblo, 1985).

7 *The Alternative Service Book 1980* (London: SPCK, 1980), pp. 230, 233.

8 The Provost of Portsmouth, Michael Yorke, held a large (and not entirely quiescent) congregation gently spell-bound by a sermon at a baptismal Eucharist on 1 September 1996 in Portsmouth Cathedral when he spoke of these four themes and applied them to the Christian life.

9 P. G. A. Robinson, 'Baptism in Ritual Perspective: Myth, Symbol and Metaphor as Anthropological Foundations for a Baptismal Theology', Durham University Ph.D., 1997, pp. 256 ff.; see also James Fernandez, *Persuasions and Performances: The Play of Tropes in Culture* (Bloomington: Indiana University Press, 1986), pp. 20–3. It was my privilege to act as external examiner for this thesis.

10 Robinson, 'Baptism in Ritual Perspective', p. 257.

11 See, for example, R. L. Wilken, 'The Interpretation of The Baptism of Jesus in the Later Fathers', *Studia Patristica* 11 (2) 1972, pp. 268–77; and Kilian McDonnell, OSB, 'Jesus' Baptism in the Jordan', *Theological Studies* 56 (1995), pp. 209–36; referred to by Robinson. See also Kilian McDonnell, OSB, *Jesus' Baptism in the Jordan: The Trinitarian and Cosmic Order of Salvation* (Collegeville: Liturgical Press, 1996).

12 J. E. L. Oulton, *Holy Communion and Holy Spirit* (London: SPCK, 1951), p. 143. I am indebted to H. R. McAdoo for drawing my attention to this work.

13 See Oliver C. Quick, *The Christian Sacraments* (London: Nisbet & Co., 1932), p. 12. I am indebted to Christopher Cocksworth for suggesting the term 'symbolic relationalism'.

14 See Dominic E. Serra, 'The Blessing of Baptismal Water at the

Paschal Vigil', *Worship* 64.1 (1990), pp. 142–56; here the new Roman Catholic Blessing of Water at the Easter Vigil is compared with its predecessor, and evidence is produced to demonstrate this contention, and also the way in which the image of rebirth has been under-played.

15 T. F. Torrance, 'The One Baptism Common to Christ in His Church', in *Theology in Reconciliation: Essays Towards Evangelical and Catholic Unity in East and West* (London: Chapman, 1975), p. 83 (whole essay pp. 82–105).

16 See Sherwin Bailey, *Sponsors at Baptism and Confirmation: an Historical Introduction to Anglican Practice* (London: SPCK, 1952); written in the diocese in which I was born, and dedicated to the bishop who confirmed me.

17 See David Holeton, *Infant Communion Then and Now*, Grove Liturgical Study 27 (Bramcote: Grove Books, 1981); Ruth A. Meyers, ed., *Children at The Table: The Communion of all the Baptised in Anglicanism Today* (New York: Church Hymnal Corporation, 1995).

18 See, especially, Avis, *Anglicanism and the Christian Church*, pp. 300 ff.

19 P. G. Lindhardt, *Grundtvig: An Introduction* (London: SPCK, 1951); A. M. Allchin, 'N. F. S. Grundtvig: The Spirit as Life-Giver', in *The Kingdom of Love and Knowledge: The Encounter between Orthodoxy and the West*, A. M. Allchin, ed., (London: Darton, Longman & Todd, 1979), pp. 71–89; Christian Thodberg and Anders Pontoppidan Thyssen, eds., *N. F. S. Grundtvig: Tradition and Renewal* (Copenhagen: Det Danske Selskab, 1983); *A Grundtvig Anthology: Selections from the Writing of N. F. S. Grundtvig (1783–1872)*, Niels Lyne Jensen, ed., (Cambridge: James Clarke, 1984); A. M. Allchin, D. Jasper, J. H. Schjørring, and K. Stevenson, eds., *Heritage and Prophecy: Grundtvig and the English-Speaking World* (Århus: University Press, 1993, and Norwich: Canterbury Press, 1993). See also Stevenson, *Handing On*, pp. 83–99.

20 See Thodberg's essay in *Heritage and Prophecy: Grundtvig and the English-Speaking World*, pp. 133 ff.

21 'Her ser du, over dåben/Gudshusets dør står åben', in *Den Danske Salmebog* (København: Haase, 1958), no. 122. I am indebted to Donald Allchin for drawing my attention to this hymn; see

also A. M. Allchin, *N. F. S. Grundtvig: An Introduction to His Life and Work* (Århus: University Press, 1997, and London: Darton, Longman & Todd, 1997), especially pp. 287ff. for a discussion of Grundtvig's defence of the sign of the cross, similar to Hooker and Taylor.

22 See *Initiation Services* GS1152C (London: Church House, 1997).

Bibliography

Primary sources

The Alternative Service Book 1980, London: SPCK, 1980

Ambrose, *In Lk*

Andrewes, Lancelot, *Ninety-Six Sermons by Lancelot Andrewes*, Library of Anglo-Catholic Theology, Oxford: Parker, 1841

—— *The Preces Privatae of Lancelot Andrewes Bishop of Winchester*, tr. and intro. F. E. Brightman, London: Methuen, 1903

A Petition for Peace: With the Reformation of the Liturgy as it was presented to the Right Reverend Bishops by the Divines appointed by His Majesties Commission, London, 1661

Augustine, *Confessions*, tr. and intro. Henry Chadwick, Oxford: Clarendon Press, 1991

—— *Ep.*

—— *Sermones*

—— *Tract. in Jn*

Baxter, Richard, *The Poetical Fragments of Richard Baxter*, London: Pickering, 1821

—— *The Practical Works of the Reverend Richard Baxter*, ed. W. Orme, London: Duncan, 1830

—— *The Reformed Pastor*, ed. William Brown, intro. James Packer, Edinburgh: Banner of Truth Trust, 1979

—— *The Works of Richard Baxter*, ed. W. Orme, London: Duncan, 1838

The Book of Common Prayer, New York: Church Hymnal Corporation and Seabury Press, 1979

Bramhall, John, *The Works of John Bramhall*, Library of Anglo-Catholic Theology, Oxford: Parker, 1842

Breward, Ian, ed., *The Westminster Directory*, Grove Liturgical Study 21, Bramcote: Grove Books 1980

Cartwright, Thomas, *A Replie to an Answere made by M. Doctor Whitgift against the Admonition to the Parliament*, 1573
—— *The Rest of the Second Replie*, 1577

Den Danske Salmebog, København: Haase, 1958

Fincham, Kenneth, ed., *Visitation Articles and Injunctions of the Early Stuart Church*, vol. 1, Church of England Record Society, Bury St Edmunds: Boydel Press, 1995

Fisher, J. D. C., *Christian Initiation: The Reformation Period: Some early Reformed rites of Baptism and Confirmation and other Contemporary Documents*, Alcuin Club Collections 51, London: SPCK, 1970

Frere, W. H., ed., *Visitation Articles and Injunctions of the Period of the Reformation*, vol. III, Alcuin Club Collections 16, London: Longmans, 1910

Gibson, Edgar, ed., *The Thirty-Nine Articles of The Church of England explained with an Introduction by Edgar Gibson*, vol. II, London: Methuen, 1897

Grundtvig, N. F. S., *A Grundtvig Anthology: Selections from the Writing of N. F. S. Grundtvig (1783–1872)*, Cambridge: James Clarke, 1984

Herbert, George, *The English Poems of George Herbert with a Priest to the Temple and his Collection of Proverbs called 'Jacula Prudentium'*, The Ancient & Modern Library of Theological Literature, London: Griffith, Farran Oakden & Welsh, n.d.
—— *The Poems of George Herbert*, with an Introduction by Arthur Waugh, Oxford: Oxford University Press, 1907
—— *The Works of George Herbert*, ed. with commentary F. E. Hutchinson, Oxford: Clarendon Press, 1941

Hilton, Walter, *The Scale of Perfections*, ed. and intro. Evelyn Underhill, London: Watkins, 1948

Hooker, Richard, *The Folger Library Edition of the Works of Richard Hooker*, Medieval and Renaissance Texts and Studies, New York: Binghampton, 1993
—— *Laws of Ecclesiastical Polity, The Works of that Learned and Judicious Divine Mr Richard Hooker*, (arranged by John Keble, revised by R. W. Church and F. Paget) II, Oxford: Clarendon Press, 1887

Isidore of Seville, *De officiis ecclesiasticis*

Jewel, John, *The Works of John Jewel*, Parker Society, Cambridge: Cambridge University Press, 1848

Langland, William, *The Vision of Piers Plowman*, ed. A. V. C. Schmidt, Everyman's Library, London: Dent, 1987

Maurice, F. D., *The Kingdom of Christ*, vol. I, London: Rivingtons, 1842

The Methodist Service Book, London: Methodist Publishing House, 1975

Patrick, Simon, *The Works of Simon Patrick DD Including his Autobiography*, ed. Alexander Taylor, Oxford: Oxford University Press, 1858

Perkins, William, *The Works of that Famous and Worthy Minister of Christ in the University of Cambridge, Mr. William Perkins*, London: John Leggatt, 1626

—— *The Work of William Perkins*, ed. Ian Breward, Courtenay Library of Reformation Classics 3, Abingdon: The Sutton Courtenay Press, 1970

Prosper of Aquitaine, *Capitula Coelestini*

Select Hymns taken out of Mr Herbert's Temple and turned into the Common Metre: to be Sung in the Tunes Ordinarily Used in Church, London: Bridge, 1697

Taylor, Jeremy, *The Whole Works of the Rt Revd Jeremy Taylor*, ed. Reginald Heber, London: Rivingtons, 1848

Thorndike, Herbert, *The Theological Works of Herbert Thorndike*, Library of Anglo-Catholic Theology, Oxford; Parker, 1844

Walton, Izaak, *Izaak Walton's Life of George Herbert*, with a preface by Canon Patrick Magee, Salisbury: Perdix Press, 1988

Westminster Abbey Library Th MS

Whitgift, John, *The Works of John Whitgift*, ed. John Ayre, Parker Society, Cambridge: Cambridge University Press, 1851–3

Secondary sources

Allchin, A. M., 'Holiness in the Anglican Tradition', in Marina Chavchavadze, ed., *Man's Concern with Holiness*, London: Hodder and Stoughton, 1970, pp. 37–58

—— 'Lancelot Andrewes', in Geoffrey Rowell, ed., *The English*

Religious Tradition and the Genius of Anglicanism, Wantage: Ikon Books, 1992, pp. 145–64

—— *N. F. S. Grundtvig: An Introduction to His Life and Work*, Århus: University Press, 1997, and London: Darton, Longman & Todd, 1997

—— 'N. F. S. Grundtvig: The Spirit as Life-Giver', in A. M. Allchin, ed., *The Kingdom of Love and Knowledge: The Encounter between Orthodoxy and the West*, London: Darton, Longman & Todd, 1979

—— *Participation in God: a Forgotten Strand in Anglican Tradition*, London: Darton, Longman & Todd, 1988

—— D. Jasper, J. H. Schjørring, and K. Stevenson, eds., *Heritage and Prophecy: Grundtvig and the English-Speaking World*, Århus: University Press, 1993, and Norwich: Canterbury Press, 1993

Avis, Paul, *Anglicanism and The Christian Church: Theological Resources in Historical Perspective*, Edinburgh: T & T Clark, 1989

Bailey, Sherwin, *Sponsors at Baptism and Confirmation: an Historical Introduction to Anglican Practice*, London: SPCK, 1952

Bauckham, Richard, 'Hooker, Travers and The Church of Rome in the 1580's', *Journal of Ecclesiastical History* 29 (1978), pp. 37–50

Bolton, F. R., *The Caroline Tradition of the Church of Ireland with Particular Reference to Bishop Jeremy Taylor*, Church Historical Society, London: SPCK, 1958

Boone Porter, Harry, *Jeremy Taylor Liturgist*, Alcuin Club Collection 61, London: SPCK, 1979

Bosher, Robert S., *The Making of the Restoration Settlement: The Influence of the Laudians 1649–1662*, London: Dacre Press, 1951

Bradshaw, Paul, *The Search for the Origins of Christian Worship*, London: SPCK, 1992

Brightman, F. E., *The English Rite*, vol. II, London: Rivingtons, 1915

Cardwell, Edward, *A History of Conferences and Other Proceedings connected with the Revision of the Book of Common Prayer from the year 1558 to the year 1690*, Oxford: Oxford University Press, 1840

Chadwick, Owen, *Michael Ramsey, A Life*, Oxford: Clarendon Press, 1990

Clark, John, 'Confession and Re-formation: Walter Hilton's Sacramental Theology' in David Brown and Ann Loades, eds., *Christ: The Sacramental Word: Incarnation, Sacrament and Poetry*, London: SPCK, 1996, pp. 143–53

Clarke, Elizabeth, 'George Herbert's *The Temple*: The Genius of Anglicanism and the Inspiration for Poetry', in Geoffrey Rowell, ed., *The English Tradition and The Genius of Anglicanism*, Wantage: Ikon, 1992

Clements, R. E., *Prophecy and Covenant*, Studies in Biblical Theology 43, London: SCM Press, 1965

The Constitutions and Canons Ecclesiastical and Thirty-Nine Articles of the Church of England, London: SPCK, 1843

Cuming, G. J., *A History of Anglican Liturgy*, London: Macmillan, 1982, 2nd edn.

Davis, Horton, *Worship and Theology in England: From Andrewes to Baxter and Fox 1603–1690*, Princeton: Princeton University Press, 1975

Deshusses, Jean, *Le Sacramentaire Gregorien: ses principales formes d'après les plus anciens manuscrits romains*, I, Spicilegium Friburgense 16, Fribourg: éditions universitaires, 1971

Donaldson, Gordon, *The Making of the Scottish Prayer Book of 1637*, Edinburgh: Edinburgh University Press, 1954

Eliot, T. S., *For Lancelot Andrewes: Essays on Style and Order*, London: Faber, 1970

—— *George Herbert*, with an introduction by Peter Porter, Writers and their work, Plymouth: Northcote House Publishers, 1994

Fernandez, James, *Persuasions and Performances: The Play of Tropes in Culture*, Bloomington: Indiana University Press, 1986

Fisher, J. D. C., *Christian Initiation: Baptism in the Medieval West: A Study in the Disintegration of the Primitive Rite of Initiation*, Alcuin Club Collections 47, London: SPCK, 1965

Frere, W. H. and C. E. Douglas, eds., *Puritan Manifestoes: A Study of the Origin of the Puritan Revolt*, Church Historical Society, London: SPCK, 1907

Gerrish, B. A., *Grace and Gratitude: The Eucharistic Theology of John Calvin*, Edinburgh: T & T Clark, 1993

—— 'The Lord's Supper in the Reformed Confession', in Donald

K. Mckin, ed., *Major Themes in the Reformed Tradition*, Grand Rapids: Eerdmans, 1992, pp. 245–5

Gy, Pierre-Marie, 'The Idea of "Christian Initiation"', *Studia Liturgica* 12 (1977), pp. 172–5

—— *La liturgie dans l'histoire*, Paris: Cerf, 1990

—— 'La notion chrêtienne d'initiation', *La Maison-Dieu* 132 (1977), pp. 33–54

Harmless, William, *Augustine and the Catechumenate*, a Pueblo Book, Collegeville: The Liturgical Press, 1995

Hastings, Adrian, 'Walter Hilton', The Eighth Southwell Lecture, 1996

Holeton, David R., ed., *Growing in Newness of Life: Christian Initiation in Anglicanism Today*, Toronto: Anglican Book Centre, 1993

—— *Infant Communion Then and Now*, Grove Liturgical Study 27, Bramcote: Grove Books, 1981

Ignatieff, Michael, *The Russian Album*, London: Penguin, 1987

Initiation Services: A Report by the Liturgical Commission, GS1152, London: Church House, 1995

Jeanes, Gordon, 'A Reformation Treatise on the Sacraments', *Journal of Theological Studies* 46.1, 1995, pp. 149–190

Johnson, Maxwell, 'Liturgy and Theology', in Paul Bradshaw and Bryan Spinks, eds., *Liturgy in Dialogue: Essays in Memory of Ronald Jasper*, London: SPCK, 1993

Kavanagh, Aidan, *On Liturgical Theology*, New York: Pueblo, 1984

—— *The Shape of Baptism*, New York: Pueblo, 1974

Kelly, J. N. D., *Early Christian Creeds*, London: Longmans, 1950

Lacey, T. A., *Herbert Thorndike, 1598–1672*, London: SPCK, 1929

Levi, Peter, *Eden Renewed: the Public and Private Life of John Milton*, London: Macmillan, 1996

Lindhardt, P. G., *Grundtvig: An Introduction*, London: SPCK, 1951

Lossky, Nicholas, *Lancelot Andrewes The Preacher (1555–1626): The Origins of the Mystical Theology of the Church of England*, Oxford: Clarendon Press, 1991

Loyer, Olivier, *L'anglicanisme de Richard Hooker: Thèse présentée devant l'université de Paris III – Le I Juin 1977*, Paris: Librairie Honoré Champion, 1979

Mazza, Enrico, *Mystagogy*, New York: Pueblo, 1989

McAdoo, H. R., *First of Its Kind: Jeremy Taylor's Life of Christ, A Study in the Functioning of a Moral Theology*, Norwich: Canterbury Press, 1994

—— *The Spirit of Anglicanism: A Survey of Anglican Theological Method in the 17th Century*, London: A & C Black, 1965

McDonnell, Kilian, OSB, *Jesus' Baptism in the Jordan: The Trinitarian and Cosmic Order of Salvation*, Collegeville: Liturgical Press, 1996

Meyers, Ruth A., ed., *Children at The Table: The Communion of all the Baptised in Anglicanism Today*, New York: Church Hymnal Corporation, 1995

Miller, E. C., jr., 'The Doctrine of the Church in the Thought of Herbert Thorndike (1598–1672)', Oxford University D.Phil. Dissertation, 1990

Modern Eucharistic Agreement, London: SPCK, 1973

New, John F. H., 'The Whitgift-Cartwright Controversy', *Archiv für Reformationsgeschichte* 59 (1968), pp. 203–11

Nuttall, Geoffrey, *Richard Baxter*, London: Nelson, 1965

Ollard, S. L., 'Confirmation in the Anglican Communion', in *Confirmation or The Laying On Of Hands*, vol. I, London: SPCK, 1926, pp. 6–245

Ottley, R. L., *Lancelot Andrewes*, London: Methuen, 1894

Oulton, J. E. L., *Holy Communion and Holy Spirit*, London: SPCK, 1951

Packer, J. I., 'A Man for All Ministries: Richard Baxter 1615–1691', the St Antholin's Lectureship Charity Lecture 1991

—— 'An Anglican to Remember: William Perkins: Puritan Populariser', the St Antholin's Lectureship Charity Lecture 1996

Paget, Frances, *An Introduction to the Fifth Book of Hooker's Treatise of Laws of Ecclesiastical Polity*, Oxford: Clarendon Press, 1907.

Paul, Robert S., *The Assembly of the Lord: Politics and the Religion in the Westminster Assembly and the 'Grand Debate'*, Edinburgh: T & T Clark, 1985

Perkins, Jocelyn, *Westminster Abbey, Its Worship and Ornaments*, vol. III, Alcuin Club Collections 38, London: Oxford University Press, 1952

Quick, Oliver C., *The Christian Sacraments*, London: Nisbet & Co., 1932

Robinson, P. G. A., 'Baptism in Ritual Perspective: Myth, Symbol and Metaphor As Anthropological Foundations for a Baptismal Theology', Durham University Ph.D., 1997

Salter, Mike, *The Old Parish Churches of Shropshire*, Malvern: Folly Publications, 1992

Schmemann, Alexander, *Introduction to Liturgical Theology*, New York: St Vladimir's Press, 1975

Serra, Dominic E., 'The Blessing of Baptismal Water at the Paschal Vigil', *Worship* 64.1 (1990), pp. 142–56

Spinks, Bryan, 'Calvin's Baptismal Theology and the Making of the Strasbourg and Genevan Baptismal Liturgies 1540 and 1552', *Scottish Journal of Theology* 48 (1995), pp. 55–78

—— 'Karl Barth's Teaching on Baptism: Its Development, Antecedents and the "Liturgical Factor"', *Ecclesia Orans* 14 (1997), pp. 261–288

—— 'Luther's Timely Theology of Unilateral Baptism', *Lutheran Quarterly* 9 (1995), pp. 23–45

—— 'Two Seventeenth Century Examples of "Lex credendi Lex orandi": The Baptismal and Eucharistic Theologies and Liturgies of Jeremy Taylor and Richard Baxter', *Studia Liturgica* 21.1 (1991), pp. 165–89

Spurr, John, *The Restoration Church of England 1646–1689*, New Haven and London: Yale University Press, 1991

Stevenson, Kenneth, *Covenant of Grace Renewed: A Vision of the Eucharist in the 17th Century*, London: Darton, Longman & Todd, 1994

—— *Eucharist and Offering*, with a foreword by Mark Santer, New York: Pueblo, 1985

—— 'The eucharistic theology of Simon Patrick' in Carsten Bach-Nielsen, Susanne Gregersen and Ninna Jørgensen, eds., *Ordet, Kirken og Kulturen: Afhandlinger om Kristendelms Historie tilegnet Jakob Balling*, Åarhus: Universitets Forlag, 1993

—— *Handing On: Borderlands of Worship and Tradition*, London: Darton, Longman & Todd, 1996

—— '"Human Nature Honoured". Absolution in Lancelot Andrewes', in Martin Dudley, ed., *Like a Two-Edged Sword – The Word of God in Liturgy and History: Essays in Honour of Canon Donald Gray*, Norwich: Canterbury Press, 1995, pp. 113–38

—— 'The *Mensa Mystica* of Simon Patrick (1626–1707): A Case-Study in Restoration Eucharistic Piety' in Nathan Mitchell, and John F. Baldovin SJ, eds., *Rule of Prayer, Rule of Faith: Essays in Honor of Aidan Kavanagh O.S.B.*, a Pueblo Book, Collegeville: The Liturgical Press, 1996

—— *Nuptial Blessing: A Study of Christian Marriage Rites*, Alcuin Club Collections 64, London: SPCK, 1982

—— 'Patterns of Christian Initiation' in David R. Holeton, ed., *Growing in Newness of Life: Christian Initiation in Anglicanism Today*, Toronto: Anglican Book Centre, 1993, pp. 137–49

—— and David Stancliffe, 'Christian Initiation and Its Relation to Some Pastoral Offices', *Theology* 760 (July/August 1991), pp. 284–91

Stewart, Stanley, *George Herbert*, Twayne's English Authors' Series, Boston: Twayne Publishers, 1986

Stranks, C. J., *The Life and Writings of Jeremy Taylor*, Church Historical Society, London: SPCK, 1952

Sweet, John, *Revelation*, London: SCM Press, 1990

Sykes, Stephen, *Unashamed Anglicanism*, London: Darton, Longman & Todd, 1995

Taft, Robert F., ' "Holy Things for the saints": The Ancient Call to Communion and its response', in Gerard Austin, ed., *Fountain of Life: in Memory of Niels K Rasmussen, O.P.*, Washington: The Pastoral Press, 1991, pp. 87–102

Thodberg, Christian, and Anders Pontoppidan Thyssen, eds., *N. F. S. Grundtvig: Tradition and Renewal*, Copenhagen: Det Danske Selskab, 1983

Torrance, Alan, *Persons in Communion: Trinitarian Description and Human Participation*, Edinburgh: T & T Clark, 1996

Torrance, T. F., 'The One Baptism Common to Christ in His Church', in *Theology in Reconciliation: Essays Towards Evangelical and Catholic Unity in East and West*, London: Chapman, 1975, pp. 82–105

Tripp, David H., *The Renewal of the Covenant in the Methodist Tradition*, London: Epworth, 1969

Vidler, Alec, *The Theology of F. D. Maurice*, London: SCM Press, 1948

Wainwright, Geoffrey, *Doxology: The Praise of God in Worship, Doctrine and Life*, London: Epworth, 1980

Watson, J. R., 'George Herbert and the English Hymn', *Theology* 794 (March–April 1997), pp. 101–8

Welsby, Paul, *Lancelot Andrewes 1555–1626*, London: SPCK, 1958

Whitaker, E. C., ed., *Martin Bucer and the Book of Common Prayer*, Alcuin Club Collections 53, Great Wakering: Mayhew-McCrimmon, 1974

Wilken, R. L., 'The Interpretation of The Baptism of Jesus in the Later Fathers', *Studia Patristica* 11 (2) 1972, pp. 268–77

Williams, Rowan, 'Deification', in Gordon S. Wakefield, ed., *A Dictionary of Christian Spirituality*, London: SCM Press, 1983, pp. 106–8

Williamson, Hugh Ross, *Jeremy Taylor*, London: Dobson, 1952

Yarnold, Edward, SJ, *The Awe Inspiring Rites of Initiation: Baptismal Homilies in the Fourth Century*, Slough: St Paul Publications, 1971

—— 'Duplex Iustitia; the 16th century and the 20th', in G. R. Evans, ed., *Christian Authority: Essays in honour of Henry Chadwick*, Oxford: Clarendon Press, 1988, pp. 204–23

Yates, Nigel, *Buildings, Faith and Worship: The Liturgical Arrangements of Anglican Churches 1600–1900*, Oxford: Clarendon Press, 1991